FATHER TIME

FATHER TIME

STEVE DUIN

arnica
PUBLISHING, INC.
Portland, Oregon

Library of Congress Cataloging-in-Publication Data

Duin, Steve.
  Father time / Steve Duin.
    p. cm.
  ISBN 0-9745686-2-7 (pbk. : alk. paper)
  1. Fatherhood--United States. I. Title.

  HQ756.D768 2004
  306.874'2'0973--dc22

                              2004011200

Author photograph by Kraig Scattarella.
Cover and text design by Aimee Genter

Arnica Creative Services
3739 SE 8th Avenue #1
Portland, OR 97202

Arnica books are available at special discounts when purchased in bulk for premiums and sales
promotions, as well as for fund-raising or educational use. Special editions or book excerpts can
also be created for specification. For details, contact the Sales Director at the address above.

For my father...
And the father I gained in marriage

TABLE OF CONTENTS

FOREWORD

BY LARRY COLTON

I READ THE LAST COUPLE PARAGRAPHS of the story and shook my head in disgust. Actually, disgust isn't a strong enough word. I was pissed. Can I say that here?

It was May 30, 1995, and it was a Steve Duin column I'd just read in *The Oregonian* that had me hopping. It was titled "Play Ball: That's an Order, Not an Invitation." I hated it.

I'd been reading Duin's columns since he started writing for the paper back in 1980, first as a sports columnist, then as a political columnist, and most recently as a general interest columnist. As a rule, I liked his writing. It was a bit edgy, opinionated, and pretty dead on. I usually agreed with his slant on things, whether it was the imbecilic behavior of the Blazers, or the ineptitude of the political clowns in Salem or at City Hall.

But it wasn't just his views I admired. It was his ability as a writer. He obviously took his craft seriously. The guy could turn a sentence. I often wondered why he wasn't out there writing books and reaching for higher literary acclaim...not that there's anything wrong with being a journalist for *The Oregonian*—not at all—but he had the chops to do other things.

But when I finished reading that column back in 1995, I wanted to take back all those positive thoughts. I was convinced the guy was a major shitbird.

The column was about his experiences coaching his son's Little League team. It wasn't the first thing I'd read where he'd used his family and his parenting as the subject for his column. Nothing wrong with that. In fact, I liked them. They weren't too precious, and they pretty much reflected the beauty and battles I'd faced in raising my own two daughters. I liked the everyman feel of his stories. Until this particular one, especially the ending:

> *I'm hardest on my kid, of course. Got to be. If I cut my own some slack, the rest of the little buggers might think they could get away with something.*
> *That's why I scream at him a little louder than the rest. Drag him along when I go on scouting trips. Force him to watch* ESPN Sunday Night Baseball, *even when the Padres are on.*
> *Push him through those hitting and fielding drills again and again and again.*
> *Maybe that's why he screamed back at me the other day, "Which one of us is playing this game, Dad?"*
> *"You are," I yelled back. "And that's the problem."*
> *We're in this together, of course. I'm doing this all for him. I'm teaching him how to win. He'll learn to choke on his own time.*

So there it was. What a jerk, capturing all that's wrong with sports in America in a few short paragraphs. (Okay, it's not *all* that's wrong, not even close, but as I said earlier, it really pissed me off.) He personified the evil Little League coach, the overbearing adult who drained the fun out of games for kids in some misguided belief that he was teaching them important lessons in life. Bull-hooey. From my experience, these evil coaches are nothing but frustrated, loser athletes, trying to inject their own sorry skills and attitudes onto the innocents.

In a past life, before becoming a writer and teacher, I had played some pro ball, lucky enough to make it to The Show for what is often referred to as a cup of coffee but would actually be better described as a demitasse. After getting out of the game, I had shied away from coaching. The phone had rung a few times with offers to coach Little League or Babe Ruth League, but I'd always said no. Too many times I'd stood at the edge of a diamond and watched and listened as lame-brained coaches and parents ranted and squawked at their kids, making total fools of themselves and ruining it for the kids. I wanted no part of all that...no part of coaches like Steve Duin, or at least the Steve Duin I'd just read about in his column.

So when he called me a few weeks later and invited me to come to one of his team's practices and work with his pitchers, I was, to say the least, caught off guard. My initial reaction was to say I'd read his column, and the Red Sox and Cubs would have to play naked in the World Series before I'd come and help. But on the other hand, I was flattered. "You pitched in the big leagues," he said. "It would really be special for the kids if you showed up and gave them a few pointers on pitching."

"I'll do it under one condition," I replied. "After I give the kids a few pitching tips, you have to let me take batting practice."

You see, I always fancied myself as a good hitter, and even though it had probably been twenty years since I'd swung a bat, I figured I could go long ball at a Little League diamond and dazzle the kids. Right?

During that phone call, I didn't say anything to Duin about his sorry-ass column. I figured I'd tell him to his face...but not until after I'd gotten to hit. I even imagined getting him so mad that he'd push me, then I'd push him back. He'd take a swing, then I'd kayo him in front of the cheering players and parents. The headline the next day in *The Oregonian* would read: "Award-Winning Columnist Decked: Ex-Ballplayer Captured After Manhunt."

The Saturday I showed up to practice was damp and gray, basic Portland baseball weather. It was a park in Lake Oswego, or Lake Grove, or one of those lakey suburbs. Batting practice was already under way when I walked onto the field. Duin was pitching to the kids. The kid at bat, short, skinny and bespectacled, was—how can I put this delicately—terrible. His best shot, on the one time he connected, sailed all the way to the front edge of the infield dirt. Well, sailed isn't quite the right word...it rolled, or more precisely, limped.

"Way to go!" Duin encouraged. It was genuine. He walked off the mound and put an arm around the little guy's shoulder, then patted him on the back. "You're really getting better."

Wait a second. This was the writer who wrote about not cutting his players any slack, and quoted somebody about "life imitating the World Series."

Several more batters took their turns, and it was the same coaching every time...encouraging words, a little instruction, a gentle admonition to hustle out to the field.

Okay, now I get it. He was doing this because I was there. He probably assumed I hadn't read his column. I'd met him on a couple occasions, and he'd even written a complimentary column about a program I had started to improve writing achievement in local schools, but we were hardly comrades in literature.

I took a couple of his players aside and worked with them briefly on a couple mechanics of pitching, nothing too fancy, just basic stuff—how to grip the ball, rotate the hips, follow through. The boys were appropriately attentive, although I had the feeling all of them would rather have been at the skate park. And I would rather have been taking batting practice.

Finally, it was time. I selected a bat, my first time ever with aluminum—I'd come from the days of real wood. The bat was also about five inches too short. It felt like I was swinging a clarinet.

I was wearing tennis shoes, and with the damp and muddy field, it was impossible to dig in. Standing on the mound ready to lob a few in my direction, Duin waved his players toward right field. I hit lefty. When they moved only a little, he motioned them to move deeper. Reluctantly, they backpedaled... but not far. The farthest one was playing me at about, oh, 200 feet. If that.

"Doesn't look like they respect my power," I said.

"Should they?" Duin asked. And smugly, I might add.

His first pitch came arching in a little above belt high. I let it go.

"What was wrong with that?" he asked.

"I'll let you know when it's a strike," I answered, motioning him to put a little more juice on it. "Or was that your top speed?"

The next pitch came in on a straight line, and I swung, uncoiling from somewhere north of Bremerton. By some modern sporting miracle, the ball and aluminum collided in perfect harmony, the ball rocketing on a high trajectory out to right field, up, up and way deep, the kids turning to stare as the ball sailed over their heads, coming back to earth in what surely must have seemed to them to be another zip code.

I stepped back from the plate, soaking in the ooohhs and aaahhs.

"You got nothing, Duin," I said.

It's weird. I played baseball almost every day from the time I was five until I was twenty-seven, and the memories have become blurred, very few moments still clear in my mind. Except I can still see Duin's punky little pitch coming toward me, then the ball soaring over those Little Leaguers' heads. Some guys remember striking out Roberto Clemente or Vada Pinson, I remember going deep on Duin.

Many balks have passed since that day, and during that time, I've read probably a couple hundred more of his columns. My opinion of his writing has changed. I think he's become an even better writer. He's one of the few writers in town who consistently takes on the big boys, and does it well, sometimes pushing the dagger extra deep. He can also write pieces that'll damn near bring a tear to your eye. His story, included in this book, about his daughter

Lauren's graduation from her elementary school, should be enshrined in the Hall of Fame of Good Stories About Schools. I love reading the letters-to-the editor his stories often elicit from angry readers who think he's some wild-eyed, flaming muckraker.

But one thing has continued to nag me about him...and that's the damn article he wrote about coaching Little League *(see page 71)*. Over the years I've gotten to know him a little better than I did back then, and the Steve Duin I've come to know, while certainly a bit on the cynical and acerbic side of the ledger, doesn't strike me as a man who would be such a shithead of a coach or human being. A reading of the stories in this book will bear that out.

So finally, after all those years, I asked him about the story. "If that's the way you coached," I said, "I wouldn't let a kid of mine play for you."

He paused, choosing his words carefully. "Go back and reread the story," he said. "Maybe you won't be so dense this time."

ACKNOWLEDGMENTS

My HEARTFELT THANKS to Roby Harrington, the high-school teacher who helped me discover my voice, and the editors at *The Oregonian*—especially Jacqui Banaszynski, Therese Bottomly, Sandy Rowe and Bill Hilliard—who gave me the freedom to use it.

INTRODUCTION

OF THE ROUGHLY 3,000 COLUMNS I've written for *The Oregonian* over the last 20 years, these are the ones that still matter.

They are, almost exclusively, about my family and my odyssey as a father, the great journey of my adult life. I was 30 years old when my son, Michael, was born in 1985. Two daughters—Christina and Lauren—would follow in the next five years.

Because I was wary of the maudlin and the self-absorbed, I didn't write about our family adventures all that often. The bridge that spans these years rests on 53 fragile columns. Several of the early pieces seem clumsy and forced because, doggone it, they were. I didn't land the newspaper's Metro column—and the blessed *carte blanche* that went with it—until 1994. Earlier, I was camped out in the sports pages or on the political beat, so I was forced to pretend the family saga had a sports angle or a political hook. Witness the convenient appearance of First Lady Hillary Clinton in the story about Lauren and the LEGOs that disappeared up her nose.

Why did I want to share any of this? On one level—to borrow a pane of glass from Vladimir Nabokov's *Pale Fire*—I hoped the window into my experience would provide a mirror for yours. Yet I also believed these stories fulfilled my job description, which is to write about the things closest to my heart.

In recent years, the writing has become more difficult. As my children became more conscious of my job and self-conscious about the boundaries of their privacy, I could no longer hang our growing pains out to dry for public amusement. My wife, Nancy, remained surprisingly tolerant whenever I did. She thought she married a photographer 23 years ago. She recognized these columns as family portraits.

If so, they were candid shots. There was never time to frame the picture, adjust the shutter speed or put the sun at my back. I rarely recognized the rites of passage—that first Homecoming dance, the Thanksgiving trip to Grandpa's house, the dismantling of the swing set in the back yard—until they bowled over me. I wrote...because I was so desperate to remember.

As you read, I would encourage you not to rush. These are still newspaper columns, after all. They were meant to be absorbed, one at a time, over a cup of coffee at the Dockside or Milo's City Cafe. I still believe in the intimacy of that morning tryst with the daily paper, and I meant to convey that in each of these stories, to remind other parents that they were not alone in their panic, their frustration, their surprise, their joy...

Or the suspicion that the Holy Father brings his mercy to bear on us all. In a response to the death of Nancy's father (the epilogue of *Father Time*) Brian Doyle, editor of *Portland,* the University of Portland's Magazine, wrote to say, "Just read your heartbroken piece on your father-in-law. It's a prayer for the man."

A prayer. So it was. In these pages, it is far from the only one.

Steve Duin
April 2005

CATERING TO HER EVERY WHIM
WHILE PONDERING BREAST PUMPS
AND JACK RAMSAY

DURING THE LAST EIGHT MONTHS, pregnancy has steadily added weight to my wife Nancy's argument that I'm not carrying my fair share of the discomfort and trauma occasioned by our first child.

Determined to be sensitive to this twisted conclusion, I explored one of the books from our Prepared Childbirth class one night last week, just before the reading lights went out.

While struggling to maintain my grip on a bed I now share with four pillows and two people who can't tie their own shoes, I skimmed fitfully through the owners' manual until it suggested I ask the expectant mother about her "fantasy labor."

I would have thought it preferable to get Nancy thinking about her fantasy island, which is Bermuda. But what do I know? as an army of in-laws would say. "Nancy," I asked, poking around between the pillows for signs of life, "what's your fantasy labor?"

As mobile as a Nautilus submarine in drydock, Nancy strained to lift one eye over the corner of her *Time* magazine. "That you do it," she said, and submerged again.

No can do. But since Nancy surprised me last fall with the news that all those nights of senseless passion have finally amounted to someone, I have discovered there are definite things an expectant father can do, not only to prepare himself for the coming fury but also to promote peace, harmony and the hope of future toddlers with the mother-to-be.

May I suggest:

60 Situps Each Night—And make 'em hurt. Believe me, your stomach muscles need tightening before you are told about breast pumps. Once you see the bras pregnant women wear, you're the one who's going to need the breathing exercises.

I'm still trying to visualize this breast pump contraption. Do you really start it like you would a lawn mower? Where do you put your feet?

Contract Out Your Gardening Work—Pregnant women are not supposed to be weeding after the sixth month. Neither are they allowed to mow the lawn, change your oil or climb up on the roof to clean the rain gutters. During the final six weeks, Nancy is also under doctor's orders not to pour her own orange juice, change the television channel or move further than her fundal height to answer the telephone.

Or so I'm told.

Play the Name Game Seriously—Leave names like "Shanda" and "King" to the founder of Lear Jets. Ease off on the stupid suggestions, such as Portia, Palefire or Amoreena. This is no time to trumpet your Shakespearean scholarship, pay homage to Vladimir Nabokov or attempt to pinpoint the Elton John song that was playing in the distance on the night you fell in love.

Surrender to Her Moods—Yield to her heart's desire. Don't argue. Try to remember why this woman is all bent out of shape. She hasn't had a drink in six or seven months. You need to be her artificial stimulant.

Jack Ramsay May Not Be the Ideal Role Model—In this kind of coaching, you are not allowed to remain on one knee on the sidelines, rising now and then to bellow, "Run the floor. Get your head in the game. How many time outs do we have left?"

Any book out of the Prego Library, such as Tracy Hotchner's *Pregnancy and Childbirth*, will equip the father with more appropriate coaching skills during labor.

You are supposed to remind your wife to keep her mouth loose and relaxed between contractions and to empty her bladder every hour. You are not supposed to balk when she sits straight up in bed and says, "Let's play Parcheesi." According to Hotchner, whatever a woman in labor wants—be it backgammon, chocolate or playing cards—a woman in labor gets.

The labor coach is not supposed to pose questions that require verbal answers. Labor is no time to wonder aloud whether sex will ever be the same, or to ask, "Nance, what does it mean when the phone rings at the end of *Local Hero?*"

Say Goodbye to Europe—Why not look at the nine-month ordeal this way? We so often ache to go someplace different, foreign and exciting, to travel beyond our limited, rain-soaked frontiers. Well, pregnancy is somewhere the two of you have never been before.

It is also something else. It is the antidote to the times loneliness whispered you could not get close enough to someone.

What's inside your wife on this Mother's Day is as close as you'll ever get, not only to the woman you love, but to the wonder that is giving yourself away and getting back more than you could possibly imagine.

GROUND RULES SET EARLY
FOR SON'S ENTRY INTO
WORLD OF SPORTS

Dear coach:

One of the major scouting combines has, no doubt, informed you of the birth of my son, Michael. Go ahead and drool, I'm getting used to it.

If his vital statistics were misplaced amid all the talk of "potential," here's the tale of the tape: Eight pounds, 6 ounces at Thursday's first weigh-in. A 13 3/4-inch chest. Only 1 foot, 7 1/2 inches tall, but an incredible reach for anything with milk in it.

Can he play with pain? The kid was circumcised before he was 18 hours old. Enough said.

According to my projections, Michael will enter Little League in 1993, high school in 1999, college in 2003 and—with degree in hand—the pros in 2007. Before you pencil him into your starting lineup, however, we need to come to some sort of understanding:

I don't trust you, Coach. I don't trust you any farther than my son can throw up. For every John Thompson or Joe Paterno in the world, who care more for their players' hearts and brains than for their athletic gifts, there are a half-dozen coaches who let kids rot on the bench, communicate best with their fingers in his facemask, and consider bribery their best recruiting tool.

Like any other father, I'm worried my son will get stuck with the wrong coach. I'm afraid his heart, his competitiveness and his precious sense of fair play may fall into the hands of the next Frank Kush or Dana Kirk. That's why I've decided that before you get to play my son—at shortstop, split end or left half—you must agree to play by my rules.

If you think you may be better off negotiating with Michael's mother, be my guest. It will deepen your affection for Howard Slusher, the renowned agent. Although she is still on the disabled list after eight hours of labor, Nancy is already pausing mid-limp to coo, "We made a pretty one, didn't we?"

Determined to preserve those looks, she does not casually entertain thoughts of flying cleats, cross-checking and blind-side hits:

"My son is never playing football. And he's never going to be a catcher or a goalie. He's not going anywhere near swinging bats and flying pucks.

"Swimming's a nice sport. No diving."

Easy, coach. A few years of refereeing the kid's combat with razor-edged coffee tables, garden slugs and the shallow end of grandpa's pool, and she'll soften up. She'll realize we can't protect Michael from misguided coaches anymore than we can shield him from Republicans, *Rocky* sequels or the cutest girl in all the world.

The following are my preferred guidelines. Give a little, Coach, and you'll get a lot. My son.

—Leave the basic training to me. The kid will be well-equipped in the fundamentals. The Nerfball hoop will be in position by the end of the week. We're developing his hand-eye coordination by playing a Foosball action tape on the rare occasions when he sleeps.

We've also begun working on Michael's delivery. Last time I peeked in his Moses' basket, he was already passing gas like a pro.

—If I ever come down with Little League Father's disease, please lock me in the equipment bins of the team bus.

—On the subject of discipline: There will be limited running of the stadium steps for the sake of showing him you're the boss. There will be no wind sprints in full pads and 90-degree heat.

If you merit Michael's respect, you will be warmed by his passion. If you don't deserve it, you are entitled to my sympathy but not a bridle for his spirit. A child's desire and ability to play sports doesn't give you license to burden him with the weight of your ego or the depth of your insecurity.

Once again, you are better off leaving this part of Michael's training to his parents. We've already begun discussing discipline with the lad. We were talking to him at 3AM Sunday. An hour later, the chat was still going merrily on.

—You have my permission to remove Michael from the lineup whenever some uncoordinated kid needs his time at the plate.

—Please skip the standard sports cliches. To begin with, my son is not putting on his pants like everyone else, one leg at a time.

Whenever you attempt to make some embarrassing analogy between life on and off the field, you risk the possibility of hearing Michael laugh out loud. Who knows what he'll do if you prattle on about "giving 110 percent." Good luck preaching like George Allen or Red Auerbach to a kid who's been coached in the real eternals.

If you must quote someone in the dugout or in the huddle, how about Williams Wordsworth, who, writing on an old ball field near England's Tintern Abbey, noted, "That best portion of a good man's life (is) his little, nameless, unremembered acts of kindness and of love."

MARCH 19, 1987

IT'S HOW YOU PLAY THE GAME

Let's open with a few thoughts from Barry Lopez's *Arctic Dreams: Imagination and Desire in a Northern Landscape.*

" ... *Confronted by an unknown landscape, what happens to our sense of wealth? What does it mean to grow rich? Is it to have red-blooded adventures and to make a fortune?*

"*Or is it, rather, to have a good family life and to be imbued with a far-reaching and intimate knowledge of one's homeland?...*

"*Is it to retain a capacity for awe and astonishment in our lives, to continue to hunger after what is genuine and worthy? Is it to live at moral peace with the universe?*"

Whatever it is about the Arctic that provokes these questions in Lopez should be familiar to those of us living in the rain belt. We are forever trying to decide what it means to be rich. We ask the questions all our lives.

When we are young, it takes the form of, "What are you going to be when you grow up?" Riches and happiness are a given; we need only chart the path we will blaze across the heavens. As we grow older, the problem of focus becomes more important. There's only so much spring left in the ol' knees. There's only so much energy left to burn.

For an 8th-grade civics class, I once confessed to dreaming about three red-blooded adventures on the road to fortune: the law, writing and professional basketball. In the last 20 years, sports have lost none of their appeal as a wonderful way to acquire the riches of this world.

You get to play the games you love. You make lots of money. People always know where you are: You're on television. Can you grow any richer than that?

Let's ask around. Let's start with Kareem Abdul-Jabbar. Think about this guy. He has scored more points than anyone in the history of the National Basketball Association. The Los Angeles Lakers' center commands the respect of his peers. He earns $2 million a year without ever breaking a sweat on the defensive boards. That sounds like wealth on any landscape.

So why is Abdul-Jabbar suing his former agent, Tom Collins, for $50 million? Why is he being served papers by several other NBA players? Why did he refuse to shake hand with Denver's Alex English before a game with the Nuggets, preferring to hide on the Laker bench?

Is it to live at moral peace with the universe?

Next stop: Chris Evert. You may scratch the Lloyd. For 15 years, Chrissie has been at or near the summit of women's tennis. She is a graceful, elegant competitor, the standard by which sportswomen and sportsmen are judged. But she is, once again, separated from her husband, John Lloyd. Evert said Tuesday that they are discussing divorce, but denied reports that Lloyd has shunned a $2 million settlement for a chance at half her wealth.

Or is it, rather, to have a good family life and to be imbued with a far-reaching and intimate knowledge of one's homeland...?

And, finally, Gary McLain. Two years ago, he was the point guard on a Villanova team that defeated Georgetown to win the National Collegiate Athletic Association basketball tournament. You couldn't buy an experience like this. His was the stuff of dreams. He was the quarterback of a monumental upset with the world looking on. How high can you get?

Not high enough for Gary McLain. Before Villanova played Memphis State in the national semifinals, he slipped into a bathroom in a motel and did a quarter-gram of cocaine. He played—literally and as usual—out of his mind.

Is it to retain a capacity for awe and astonishment in our lives, to continue to hunger after what is genuine and worthy?

What does it mean to grow rich? If the meaning has temporarily escaped Abdul-Jabbar, Evert and McLain, perhaps that is because they are dealing with the riches of this world. We were warned long ago about treasures on earth, "where moth and rust destroy, and where thieves break in and steal."

Does sport provide the meaning of storing up the treasures of heaven? Speaking Tuesday night to the young athletes at West Hills Christian School, I suggested three ways of playing for the riches that endure:

- Treasure the company of friends. The happiest times I've ever known on the basketball court have been spent with three college buddies. I don't remember winning and losing with them; I just remember playing together. Working toward a common goal never has been so simple. When I am with these friends, I am rich beyond my understanding. Treasure such company.

- Don't place too much trust in the thrill of victory or the agony of defeat. And don't take either too seriously. Whether you are celebrating or grieving a one-point or one-run decision, don't hold the pose too long.

- Keep your eyes open for the presence of God. Some folks believe that if God attends sporting events, it's only to sit atop the scoreboard and manipulate the final result. Losers shrug and say, "I guess that was God's will." Winners mistake a surge of adrenalin for a heavenly boost.

I doubt it. But I suspect God is always there, beckoning you forward to comfort someone crushed by defeat. He's nudging you toward the opponent bruised by your temper, reminding you that your self-worth hasn't increased or decreased according to the final score—preserving the riches you store up for Him.

JANUARY 24, 1988

COUNTDOWN TO FEAR

W E WERE CHANNEL-SCANNING, my son and I, rolling along the television dial from MTV to CNN, and back again. Michael was on my arm, a small, lingering fever showing in the blush on the cheek he had resting on my shoulder. On we rode together, going nowhere in particular on a gloomy winter afternoon, skipping from channel to channel until I stumbled over the last flight of the *Challenger.*

I stopped to watch, surprised by a slightly different angle of that January morning two years gone. A cameraman, possibly one from Lauderdale or Coco Beach, perhaps even Christa McAuliffe's hometown in New Hampshire, had decided to film the launch from the spectator gallery at Cape Canaveral. This was his prize-winning footage. As the shuttle lurched slowly into that royal blue sky, he panned over the faces turned heavenward, the faces of fathers and mothers, of students and friends. Dawning on each were the first lines of all the stories they would tell.

For several moments, the *Challenger* rose in a frightfully glorious arc, its train a plume of clear, white smoke. Then the picture changed, and we had the shuttle in familiar close-up, eight miles high. "Go at throttle up," Dick Scobee, the flight commander, said, just before that burst of gleaming light.

Michael began to squirm. He lifted his head off my shoulder and brought one hand to his mouth. At the age of 2 1/2, he still takes what he sees on television literally, and he's easily disturbed by fist fights or chase scenes or an unexpected disappearing act. "What happened?" he asked, peering at the mushrooming cloud. "What'd it do?"

Only then did I remember that, nearing their second anniversary, my son had never seen these pictures before. There was nothing obvious about NASA's "major malfunction" for him. On the morning it happened—two years ago this Thursday—Michael was at Emanuel Hospital, undergoing surgery to remove a bronchial cleft from his throat.

It was a simple operation, Dr. Timothy Campbell had assured us, but that didn't mean something couldn't go wrong with the anesthesia. The anesthesiologist had called us at home the night before to remind us. One time in 50, one in a 100, you just never know.

Michael was entranced by the anesthesiologist's glasses as he was carried to the operating room. He was gone a long time. I had just reminded my wife, Nancy, not to worry when the phone rang in our waiting room. Bad news, I thought, even as the nurse picked up the phone.

It was her daughter, calling from home. In the fragile silence of that room, we caught only small pieces of the conversation. "Oh, that's terrible... the one the school teacher was on...? I know, dear, I know you just had to tell someone."

When the nurse hung up the phone, she said, yes, something had happened to the space shuttle, just after takeoff. We were sitting there, locked in our disbelief, when Dr. Campbell wheeled around the corner and told us everything was fine. We'd have our son back in 30 minutes.

Before Michael returned, wailing in rasping rage at the bandages on his throat and the IV tubes taped to his wrist, we must have watched the replay of the *Challenger*'s final flight a dozen times.

"What'd it do?" Michael asked again. What'd it do? On an unusually cold launch morning at Cape Canaveral, the inevitable and the inexplicable collided. The booster seals failed, as some minor engineers at Morton Thiokol guessed they eventually would. One time in 50, you just never know. Two years later, those engineers are still testing solid fuel rockets in the desert. They still don't know if they can keep it from happening again.

"Daddy, listen to me," Michael said sternly, his hands on either side of my face. "What'd it do?"

I had the beginnings of tears in my eyes. Knowing they would frighten him, I held them back. Those tears were as much for what can go awry when seven people are flung into space as when a 6-month-old boy is rendered unconscious and surrendered to providence and a doctor's hands. All that can go wrong. All that did. All that didn't.

"It exploded," I told my son. He nodded absently, trustfully, and returned his fevered cheek to my shoulder.

NOVEMBER 27, 1988

UNSPEAKABLE GRATITUDE

ONE MORNING IN EARLY NOVEMBER, the intercom in our bedroom began to rattle and hum two hours before my alarm clock did. My daughter, Christina, had wearied of sleeping alone and was calling for room service.

She was waiting at crib's edge, reaching first for me and then for the bottle of warm milk in my bathrobe pocket. In a few moments, we were all wrapped up in one another in the rocking chair, coasting in the darkness. Christina was wedged between my left arm and my heart, tracing the ridge of my eye with one outstretched finger, when I remembered my Thanksgiving column.

For the last four years, I have written on this holiday weekend of the people and events that left me numb with gratitude. Writing on the sports page of *The Oregonian,* I dished out my appreciation to those rare exceptions to the rule that athletes are overpaid, ill-humored, self-centered brats. I paid tribute to the warmth of Stu Inman and the principles of Rick Bay. I reminisced about the comic genius of Mychal Thompson and one memorable final round at the Masters with Jack Nicklaus.

Each column was harder to write than the last. I blame it on the kids. The more I care about them, the less I care about the games strangers play, no matter how well they play them.

Since Michael and Christina initiated their friendly takeover of my life, my giving of thanks has been more conducive to sighs than proclamations. I am a little embarrassed to go public with what I am most thankful for. The words I would speak, if I could find them, weren't made to be tossed around.

When Christina calls for me to come and rock the night away, the comfort we take in each other is, I trust, familiar to most fathers and daughters, and sounds pretty maudlin to everyone else. Don't worry: I'm not inviting anyone to share the moment. There's only enough warm milk for one, and enough mystery for two. Only when Christina has grown old enough to serve herself, or too self-conscious for my lap, will I grow desperate enough to put words to the message she was tracing on my face in the dark.

Some of the things that are most dear to us are protected by a similar vow of silence. When we are cut by remorse, or stabbed by romance, we bleed in private. That was brought home to me several months ago when a man named Al Holbert died alone in a single-engine airplane crash in Pennsylvania.

He was a gentle, introspective soul and a brilliant race car driver, a gift he'd shared many times over the years at Portland International Raceway. Each time he returned, we sought shelter in the racing pits and sat and talked like old friends, usually about things far more compelling than racing and sports writing.

I was sitting at the kitchen table with the Sunday paper when I read the brief story about Holbert's death. My first thought was to go down to the office and write something about him. He deserved an epitaph, a public fanfare for a life that made a difference. But by the time my kids popped out of bed, and came searching for oatmeal, I knew I couldn't write it. Whatever the right words, my heart wasn't about to give them up.

So I went alone to church, the early service, and sat quietly and self-contained until the piano player laid his hands on a song that always leaves its fingerprints on my throat. The why of that is so deep within me that I can't pull it out. But as the piano played, and those around me sang, I wrote my goodbyes to Al Holbert, in words that couldn't bear repeating.

I bled in private, and then went home, desperate for my daughter. When she heard my key in the front door, she came running for me, her arms and mine outstretched in breathless, speechless reunion.

BLESS THE BEASTS
AND THE CHILDREN

THIRTY SECONDS AFTER WE ENTER Alley Cat Pets, the raucous barking begins. My daughter, Christina, pops the first cork, greeting a 3 1/2-month-old Australian shepherd as if they were old friends. He cocks his head, trying to make the connection, while Christina continues to serenade him.

My son, Michael, ignores the ruckus and heads straight for the sailfin and brown water dragons. The lizards are eyeing the parakeets, sizing up their clipped wings and dreaming the impossible dream, but Michael is a lot more curious about the Odor Free Pet Odor Eliminator aerosol can on the ledge by the dragon cage. Unlike his 20-month-old sister, Michael is pretty pragmatic about our pet shop visits. He knows not to fall in love with anyone that moves. We're just visiting, after all. We didn't bring an extra car seat for the Persian kitten with the $200 sticker.

Michael has already gotten the pet lecture. I think "not in this lifetime" were my exact words. At 3 1/2 , he's only half as old as he needs to be to practice safe, responsible pets. So he concentrates on the inanimate objects. One day it's the Resco jumbo animal nail trimmer, the next it's the boxes of Super Ick cure with nitrofurazone ("Kills the parasite, heals the wound").

Today, it's the odor eliminator and the Hot Tamales gumball machine. Michael is staring into the belly of the beast and, I assume, screaming for my spare change. I can't make out his exact words. The Australian shepherd has finally placed Christina, and their barking duet has loosed the gerbils from their sound, endless sleep.

Fred Gray is paying us no mind. He's never complained about our visits, for he has an abiding faith that if we keep coming back, and keep pretending that one hour a week is sufficient communion in this zoo, one of his animals will finally end up in my daughter's arms. Abiding faith is a prerequisite when you own a pet store, particularly one in a Tigard strip mall. You have to trust that the 7-week-old Sheltie that just went out the door isn't going to spend its life on a dirty bedspread in some garage.

"The couple who bought that dog, they waited until she quit work," Gray tells me. "People are becoming more aware that these are living souls that require some care."

How much care depends on the pet. Dogs want to run your life, of course. Cats are always in court, seeking a restraining order that will bar you from the house. Most of the pets in between—fish, birds, turtles, rabbits—are relatively bored by the human comedy. Apparently, that's part of their appeal. "Fish have become quite a psychological tension reliever," Gray says. "People sit around and watch fish swim back and forth."

I beg Gray's pardon for a moment. Michael is peering into the goldfish tanks, his nose quivering. "What's that smell?" he asks me. "Lifetime imprisonment," I say. At my feet, Christina has discovered a pregnant cat lounging on the feline equivalent of a beanbag chair. She gets down on her knees, lowers her cheek to the cat's belly as if listening to the babies move, and wraps the animal in a heartfelt embrace.

"Are you giving the kitty-cat a hug?" I say. The cat rolls her eyes, trying not to gag, even as Christina laughs and, trying to stand up, kicks the cat square in the face. The cat quickly takes refuge beneath the shelf holding the giant plastic bags of wood chips, while Christina, still bubbling with desire, drops to her belly and tries to wriggle after her.

"We don't sell snakes," Gray chips in. "We don't sell spiders, and we don't sell snakes." Some people won't come in the store if there are snakes, he explains, but that's only part of the reason.

Snakes are a different kind of psychological tension reliever, you see. Gray doesn't mind that some of his merchandise are hors d'oeuvres at the neighborhood deli counter. He probably sells 1,500 feeder goldfish a week. "A 14-inch oscar will go through a couple dozen goldfish a day," he says. Neither does he sweat the crickets. Every week, another 500 crickets show up in a cardboard box from some cricket farm in California or Boise. Lizard and spider food. Nothing else.

But with snakes, it's different. Some snake owners will take anything that cowers in a corner home for dinner. They love the rats. Gray, who's proud to say that he's never had to discard one of his dogs or cats at a pound, tries not to get too attached to the rats. "I suffer more," he tells me, "when people take gerbils and hamsters for their snakes."

Gray pulls from its cage a small white rat, which burrows into the warm cave of his hands. "Rats make the best pets for a kid you can find," he says. "They like people. They're sociable, they're friendly." What's more, they can sleep by your bed without hogging the pillow.

I look at Christina and look at the rat, then shake my head. I can't picture them together. Gray nods and returns the rat to its cage. It's OK. He has this abiding faith that our time will come. He knows it won't be the Fischer lovebirds or the alligator gars or one of the Amazon parrots that act as though they own the place. But one of these days, he figures, my daughter and some puppy will bark in perfect harmony, and my heart won't be able to take the strain of pulling them apart.

Michael could tell Fred a thing or two—I think "not in this lifetime" might be his exact words—but at the moment he's knee-deep in the cat toys, holding them spellbound with the story of his life.

SEPTEMBER 6, 1990

KINDERGARTEN IS ONLY
THE FIRST COURSE

MY SON, MICHAEL, returned from his first day of kindergarten Tuesday bummed to the max.

What's the problem, I asked?

"Let's play baseball," Michael said.

In a minute. Tell me what went wrong.

"Nothing," he said, shrugging. "I just thought that all I really would need to know about how to live and what to do and how to be I would learn in kindergarten."

Whatever gave you that asinine idea?

Michael pointed to the poster on his bedroom wall, the one with the big red apple and the theology of Robert Fulghum. "Well, that's what the sign says."

Your mother bought that, I said. You've never caught me reading that poster to you before you go to bed.

Michael twisted this thought for a moment. "You mean it's not true?" he asked.

I'm afraid not, I said. Kindergarten isn't all it's cracked up to be. Little of what you really need to know about how to live and what to do and how to be will come to you at the age of 5.

"Name one thing," Michael said. "Name one thing I won't learn if I go to kindergarten every day."

C'mere, I said, pulling Michael into my lap. Now, pay attention:

Remember all the parents who showed up with video cameras when you got on the bus this morning? Don't be fooled. Very little of your life will be spent on camera. And what really counts is how you behave when you're sure no one is watching.

You lose your job if you take a nap after lunch.

Playing fair and passing up the chance to hit people is all well and good, but it's no way to get elected.

When you're on the playground, watching all your buddies on the swings, every one of them looks capable of soaring like an eagle. Don't be fooled. When some of those kids grow up, they'll be sorting albums in a record store. And that's exactly where they belong.

Nothing makes as much sense as LEGOs.

If you sit in one place long enough, people stop asking you to move. Incumbents prove this all the time.

Now is not the time to try to explain how complicated this business about wearing your rubbers is going to get.

The biggest word of all may be, "Look!" but what the Dick-and-Jane books won't tell you is that the slyest instinct is, "Take!"

Few people in the world will ever spend as much time looking out for you as your kindergarten teacher.

You can't eat everything you want.

Goldfish and hamsters and white mice, and even the little seed in the Styrofoam cup, will indeed all die. Much harder to kill are Canadian thistle, grudges and rumors about politicians and marital infidelity. No one knows why this is so.

Actually, someone knows. God knows. But they aren't allowed to talk to you about God in kindergarten.

When you punch holes in a piece of construction paper, you prove capable of a task beyond the talents of most grown-ups: voting.

The Cubs will never win the pennant.

Remember that little boy on the bus who was screaming at you to get off at the wrong stop? You're going to meet a lot more counselors like him, and too many of them will try to fool you by whispering, as if theirs is a secret you can't live without.

Few who have made a difference in this century have wasted a single minute thinking about what a better world it would be if we all had cookies and milk about three o'clock every afternoon and then lay down with our blankies for a nap.

Always write thank-you notes.

And while you have that pen out, write your name on everything you see, like the senators and congressmen do. That way no one can accuse you of taking something that isn't yours.

Few people handle their wealth as well as Uncle Scrooge.

You are one of Rep. Ron Wyden's constituents.—Now, now. Sometimes crying does do you a world of good.

Someday soon, you're going to have to make your own lunch.

When you go out into the world, you can't possibly avoid all the traffic. So, wear a helmet, but on your head, not over your heart.

Michelangelo, Leonardo, Raphael and Donatello were real people before they became heroes in a halfshell.

If you really want to go out into the backyard and play baseball, keep telling your dad you want to be the next Bobby Bonilla. Your dreams are now just as precious as his own.

AUGUST 4, 1991

GOING, GONE TO THE OL' BALL GAME

BALTIMORE

When the Orioles' Dwight Evans came to bat in the seventh recently with the bases loaded and Baltimore trailing Oakland 9–5, Matthew Kopetski turned to his father—and his congressman—and solved the deficit problem:

"Now, if he homers, the score is tied," Matthew said.

Evans wiggled his left foot at some junk, then chased a chest-high fastball. He caught it, too, fair and square, driving the ball into the left-field bleachers, 20 feet inside the foul pole.

Before the ball reached its apex, 43,000 Oriole fans were on their feet, roaring their relief.

Rep. Mike Kopetski, D-Ore., and his son rose with them. I hoisted my 6-year-old son aloft so he could share in the celebration that rocked Memorial Stadium. He watched Evans circle the bases and listened to the rapture, and I could tell he was struggling to connect the dots.

"A home run," I said. "Grand slam."

"Where did it go?" Michael asked.

I pointed to the orange derrick towering above the left-field corner. "Just inside the foul pole."

"Inside the foul pole!" Michael exclaimed, squirming for a better view of this slam dunk. I needed another inning and a half—and several diagrams on our game program—to convince Michael the ball hadn't disappeared inside the foul pole, only breezed by on its fairest side.

You will forgive my son's confusion. This was his first major-league game. It was also the first for Matt Kopetski, who had to wait 15 years for his dad to take him out to the ball park.

"This is history," the congressman said when we rolled down off Capitol Hill and headed north. This was a night to remember. For the last quarter-century, our best memories of the game were sparse and remote, like the time when a catcher's game-winning hit in Pendleton produced the headline in the *East Oregonian,* "Kopetski Breaks up Game." At long last, we were breaking new ground and sharing the game with our sons.

The trip to the ballpark was a luxury for Kopetski, who hasn't had time to catch his breath, much less a foul ball, since he sent Mr. Smith back to Oregon.

"That's the toughest thing about the political life," Kopetski said. "There isn't enough time." Almost every weekend, he red-eyes back to the district to raise money (Kopetski has less than $15,000 set aside for his next campaign) or grab a conspicuous seat at the annual Possum Festival. Since his election, Kopetski has spent more evenings at the Boston home of John Kenneth Galbraith (one) than at the home of the Orioles.

Galbraith advised the freshman congressman to read daily something more substantial than *The New York Times.* On this night, Kopetski opted for an Orioles' program and a lineup card.

It was Bat Night, and the 3,000th game played at Memorial Stadium, a weary old dame that will lose the Birds next year to a new park. "History. Like I said," Kopetski reminded me.

Neither of us can claim that heredity is responsible for our sons' intense allegiance to the game. Kopetski is a Cardinal fan, but Matt likes the Yankees. Given the chance, I would have passed the Washington Senators down to Michael; instead he adores the Pirates, an affection that owes more to his LEGOs than Bobby Bonilla. Both kids are rabid collectors of baseball cards; both fathers are appalled that the card companies so shamelessly churn out worthless "collector's items."

There ought to be a law, I said. "Maybe I can have the GAO do a study," Kopetski mused.

If the feds ever want to balance the budget, they should take over the ball-park concessions. Aided by a rain delay, Kopetski and I shelled out $50 for peanuts, pizza and Cracker Jacks, and cotton candy as sticky as the night air.

Matt and Michael consumed it all. They witnessed two grand slams and Rickey Henderson steal one base and get nailed going for a second. They got to see one of the game's most unassuming stars, Cal Ripken Jr., and one of its most pretentious, Jose Canseco.

"Dad, why does it say 'Big Jerk' on the back of his uniform?" Michael asked.

Hey, it was his first game. By the time he figures out it doesn't, he'll realize it should.

In the top of the ninth, several minutes past midnight, Oakland scored three runs to take a 12-9 lead. We lingered until the final out, on the chance that the unexpected would lift us above the hour, the night, the peanut shells and spilt Cokes.

On the drive back to Washington, Michael fell asleep atop his bat and baseball cards, his weary feet in Matt's lap.

Closer to the dashboard lights, their fathers dreamed about a world in which their sons would have more time at the ballpark than they ever did. More cuts at the plate, and more chances to break up the game.

FEBRUARY 28, 1993

DEAR HILLARY:
BEWARE THAT LEGO-ECTOMY

I<small>F</small> HILLARY RODHAM CLINTON TRULY WANTS to tackle the high cost of health care, she better be prepared for the $1,800 LEGO.

And let's hope she—unlike my 2-year-old daughter—doesn't inhale.

One afternoon in early January, Lauren arrived at my knee and politely informed me that one of her older brother's LEGOS had disappeared.

In a house containing at least 20,000 LEGOs, this didn't strike me as a significant loss. "Where did it go?" I asked, trying to sound paternal and concerned.

"Up my nose," Lauren replied.

That was my cue, of course, to call Lauren's mother. Unfortunately, my wife, Nancy, wasn't home. I was on my own. Peering inside Lauren's delicate, midget nostrils, I didn't see a thing.

Not the strut from the Galactic Peace Keeper or the parrot from Shipwreck Island. Not even Black Monarch's Ghost.

But Lauren was adamant. She'd stuffed a LEGO up her nose and she was still waiting for her nose to give it back.

A half-hour later, we finally had an official sighting: A red plastic LEGO taillight—about a quarter-inch wide—was way back in sinus country. I had the flashlight and tweezers out when Nancy got home. She quickly decided the emergency room at St. Vincent's was a much better idea, and off we went.

At the hospital, we got a rousing reception. Lauren's stuffed nose was a nice, relaxed change of pace from the usual blood and cuts.

But no one could reach the taillight. When the doctor asked Lauren to blow her nose, she took a deep breath...and the little sucker vanished.

Next stop: day surgery. That surgery, I hasten to add, went well. When Jay Richards, the anesthesiologist, was introduced to Lauren in the waiting room, she called him "a butthead," but he was kind enough to send her to dreamland and bring her back without a hitch.

Dr. Paul Kaplan—the ear, nose and throat specialist—and his grasping forceps took care of the rest in less than 20 minutes. He returned the LEGO and our little girl in separate bundles, and we were home free.

Well, not exactly. In the next month, the bills began to trickle in. That visit to the emergency room cost $180.45.

Richards' fee? $462.

Kaplan's? $383.

And St. Vincent's fee for the "ambulatory surgical care," the use of the recovery room, and generally seeing us through all the muss and fuss?

$771. On the nose.

The total cost of separating Lauren and that LEGO came to $1,796.45.

For quite a few families, $1,800 would amount to one hefty health-care crisis. We can afford to laugh about all this only because we have Blue Cross. Most of the bills for Lauren's trip to LEGOland are 100 percent deductible under *The Oregonian's* insurance plan.

Now, you figure someone must be getting rich off this racket, and your first guess is probably the doctors involved.

I'm in no mood to give those doctors grief, not after they gave me back my daughter happy and whole. In any event, Richards said the doctors receive only 18 cents of each dollar billed.

The rest disappears—like a LEGO taillight—into overhead, local taxes, spendy supplies, Blue Cross discounts, cost-shifting (that is, paying for the treatment of those who have no insurance) and liability insurance.

"Our current system tends to reward the providers of service and severely punish those providers if they make an error," Kaplan said. That system also provides relatively painless choices to those who have a Blue Cross card in their wallet, and rations the pain to those who don't.

If your priority is saving money, Kaplan added, you could have a less-experienced anesthesiologist on hand. Ninety-nine times out of a 100, you wouldn't have a problem. You could also cut back on the support staff that hangs out in the operating room, just in case something goes wrong.

But if your priority is your daughter, a fragile little girl with a curious nose... One LEGO-ectomy adds up to $1,800.

"Is this an outrageous amount of money? It sure is," Kaplan said. "On the other hand, it sure is your daughter. How much suffering and lack of care are you willing to tolerate to have a better bottom line?

"That's the decision Hillary Clinton is going to have to help us make."

And I hope she helps us before my daughter gets a good whiff of her Duplos.

AMAZING FAITH

S ARAH IS STILL...

Still with us. Still speechless. Still blind.

"I still set the alarm clock in the hallway," says her mother, Kathleen Huserik. "I still get up at one, four and six in the morning.

"Still put the tent over her at night. Still play the harp music at bedtime."

When Sarah Huserik was born 10 years ago, two months before her lungs or her crib were ready, no one knew how soon the stillness would catch up to her. Unsure if she would survive a year, her parents, Chris and Kathleen Huserik, celebrated her birthday on the 28th of each month.

In March, 10 legitimate candles were on her cake. Sarah has overcome brain seizures and heart disease and muscle disorders and laser surgeries and that ever-present gastrostomy tube. She weighs almost 80 pounds and her braided hair falls to her waist, but she is, as her mother once said, the eternal newborn. Sarah is as helpless as the day she was born.

For 10 years, she has been in diapers, in distress, indefatigable.

You'd think her mother, still rising twice each night and again at dawn to suction the fluid from Sarah's lungs, would need a break, but no one has ever heard Kathleen, 37, ask for one. It is one of the mysteries of this child's life. Sarah is an endurance test. She has pushed her caretakers past the cusp of their patience to the limits of their love.

But those who have gone the distance with Sarah, who can look back over the years and can't look forward to healing, say the most amazing things.

One nurse, Lisa Childs, says Kathleen is the happiest person she has ever known. Another, Deva Harris-Williams, insists that the Huseriks' mobile home in North Plains is a joyful place to be.

These nurses can't see Sarah often enough, or work enough hours. They wouldn't miss the chance to tuck Sarah into the tent of stuffed animals and blankets that is her warm goodnight, or to listen to the harp music that invites her to rest.

They are eavesdropping on a unique faith. They're in on a perplexing secret. They know that grace abides. And where.

On a tree farm in North Plains. In the heart of a 10-year-old girl who will never speak the words of Morris West that are framed on her bedroom wall:

> *I know what you are thinking. You need a sign. What better one could I give than to make this little one whole and new? I could do it, but I will not. I am the Lord and not a conjuror. I gave this mite a gift I denied to all of you—eternal innocence. To you, she looks imperfect—but to me she is flawless, like the bud that dies unopened or the fledgling that falls from the nest to be devoured by the ants . . .*

· · ·

Sarah was 7 before they realized she was blind. "Cortically blind," Kathleen Huserik explains. "Her eyes are fine, but because of the brain damage, her brain can't process what she sees."

Only Sarah's ears warn her what's coming. If the intruder doesn't make a sound, she has no time to get ready. She is unprepared for the swatch of sunlight on her forehead or the breeze on her cheek. Too much stimulus for her brain to handle, these gentle gestures of Mother Nature are more than enough to start a seizure.

"Horror-staring," as Kathleen describes it. "Her eyes get really big, like she's watching a horror movie."

The seizures pass quickly. They are only ghosts, shadows, of the major assault that fused the circuits in her brain the night of Feb. 20, 1985.

Sarah had spent the first 11 months of her life in a 10-by-7-foot room at Emanuel Hospital. Twelve hours after she came home for the first time, seizures attacked her in her bed, and part of her was lost forever. The seizures lasted three hours. The brain waves on the electroencephalograms were never as spirited again.

If you can meet Sarah's eyes on that original cover photograph of *Northwest Magazine*, you might wince to meet them now. The brain struggles to process what you see.

There are, after all, the bulky mechanics of her life. The wheelchair. The endless hum of the ventilator that helps her breathe. The Hoyer lift that Kathleen and the nurses use to hoist her out of bed.

"It's a forklift," her mother says. Brian, Sarah's 11-year-old brother, calls it a crane. "We jack her up and put her into the chair. It saves our backs."

In the six hours each day that Sarah spends in her chair, she is wrapped inside five cloth diapers and a pair of adult plastic pants. Her hands are sometimes so cold, owing to her lack of movement, that her father warms them with the hair dryer. "She's a lot like a quadriplegic," Kathleen says. "She can't move anything purposefully."

Sarah's bones, her mother says, are as fragile as Ivory Soap: She broke her left femur last year when the leg got caught under her when she was being forklifted into bed. Sarah didn't cry out, she only winced. Kathleen didn't know anything was wrong until the next day.

"Everything that child has ever needed had to be provided," Harris-Williams says. "Before the seizures, she could indicate what she needed. She'd ring her bells or make her alarms go off on purpose. Now, you have to anticipate what she wants and what she needs."

Yet there is something about this child. Something in her eyes, which still reach for the world she can't see, and her responsive smile. "Something that draws people to Sarah," Kathleen says. Even the people who dread the thought of meeting her.

After Michele Elskamp—another of the nurses who helps Kathleen so she can attend to her full-time nursing job at Legacy Good Samaritan Hospital—brought her dad out to the farm, he couldn't stop talking about it.

"I expected this totally depressing, end-of-the-hospital-corner-room sort of thing where this kid is dying," he told Elskamp on the way home. "And she's one of the family. She has her own frilly room. She has a mom who talks to her as if she's any little kid."

Sarah isn't dying, and the Huseriks aren't dying around her. "At the start, there was more a chance of losing her," says Chris Huserik, 38. He was born to farm but continues to teach in Kenton School in North Portland for the sake of health insurance, which has covered $1.2 million in medical care over the years. "She's been stable for so long. I don't think about that now."

Her medicine chest—containing nine prescriptions, including four seizure drugs—would choke a midsized van, but there's never been another helicopter ride back to Emanuel. The nurses know they are not to perform any heroics to keep Sarah alive, and for the past nine years medical heroics haven't been necessary.

The doctors' advice comes over the phone. The nurses come to her door. And when Sarah gets them alone...

"Sarah knows more about me personally than anyone on this Earth," Elskamp says. "When the house is empty, we have the greatest talks. I'll share anything with her.

"She hates to have her face washed, hates it like any other kid. She loves it when you're beating on her chest. She loves it when you stroke her face. She loves the sound of Velcro ripping, or when the oxygen man comes and changes the oxygen tanks. She really gets off on that."

If Sarah doesn't betray her pain, she revels in her pleasures. "You can see right to her soul," says Lisa Childs. "There's not all the other stuff that people use to hide themselves."

Childs' second baby, Katie, was born with two holes in her heart, and Childs still was bitter when she met the Huseriks, two years ago. She had a tough time dealing with Sarah. Katie had open-heart surgery scheduled.

"I was afraid," Childs says, "that something would happen during surgery and Katie would end up like Sarah."

Nothing went wrong for Katie. After a week of intensive care at Emanuel, the Childs family came home. "To think the Huseriks were there for a year," Lisa says. "To see Kathleen's grace and acceptance has helped me a lot. If that were my daughter . . . I don't know how she does it. It must be a gift from God."

A half-dozen nurses moonlight at the farm. Three therapists come by to rearrange Sarah's muscles, romance her fingers and plant seeds of sensation in her brain. They all agree that nothing moves her like her mother's voice.

That's still a calm voice, a patient voice, whether Kathleen is feeding Sarah pureed leftovers, leading her through another Jane Fonda workout, or whispering in her ear, "Surely goodness and mercy will follow us all the days of our lives."

Mother and daughter are usually together. When Kathleen hears footsteps, she doesn't look back. She knows it's only goodness and mercy on their daily rounds.

• • •

...She is necessary to you. She will evoke the kindness that will keep you human. Her infirmity will prompt you to gratitude for your own good fortune. More! She will remind you every day that my ways are not yours, and that the smallest dust mote whirled in darkest space does not fall out of my hand. I have chosen you. You have not chosen me. This little one is my sign to you. Treasure her.

—MORRIS WEST

One afternoon several years ago, Michele Elskamp got word that Sarah was scheduled for another round of laser surgery.

Three previous rounds had failed to clear the abnormal tissue growth in Sarah's trachea. Her airway was 90 percent blocked and Sarah, though not in serious danger, was seriously worn out.

Elskamp rushed to the farm. "The nurses' customary thing is to give a couple of knocks and walk in the door," she says. "I ran back to Sarah's room. Chris and Kathleen were both there. It was one of those rare times that I've seen Kathleen crying."

It had been a long day, but Sarah was all right. They talked for a few more minutes, Elskamp says, "and all of a sudden Chris goes, 'Well, I think I'm going to put on some pants now.' I looked down and he's standing there in shirttails and socks."

The Huseriks aren't hung up on ceremony. Or second-guessing. Or circumstance. "The key word is acceptance," Kathleen says. In the first weeks of Sarah's life, Chris and Kathleen decided to stop grieving and to accept both their daughter and the unknown.

"To some degree, I think Sarah has defined their lives," says Ted Nordlund, a pastor at the Huseriks' church, West Hills Covenant. "They have chosen to see her as a gift. Their love and their care awaken something in her."

Eternal newborns have ripped families apart. All too often, only one of the parents can handle it. "That doesn't seem to be an option here," Chris Huserik says. Sarah and Brian needed them both. So Chris chose to work two jobs. Kathleen chose to take on much of Sarah's care and save money by arranging the nursing schedules.

After 10 years, they understand why Jesus never said a word about unanswered prayer.

"The Huseriks are only human," Elskamp says. "Anyone without God in their lives would hit the frustration peaks hard and often."

Instead, the Huseriks aim to serve. "They know every bad thing that's happened to me in the last 10 years," Harris-Williams says. "All the ups and downs. Kathleen is so supportive. A card will come in the mail. There'll be a hug at the door. There aren't many people in the world . . ."

Again and again, you hear that refrain. "I've been a nurse for eight years," Childs says, "and I've never had a boss like this before, leaving me notes and telling me they love me."

This is one of the mysteries of this child's life. Her weakness has strengthened those who love her the most. Her parents have not simply endured; they have been enriched. Their faith has not been challenged, but confirmed.

"When you are with Sarah or her mother, you are with a person who has said 'Yes!' to life when there's no reason to," Nordlund says. "When I've been with Sarah, I have my own sense of survival drawn out of me, my own sense of hope, my sense of destiny. She has never committed the sin of giving in to the limits placed upon her."

Those who have waited on Sarah all these years now share her secret. On the day she turned 10, they gathered around her on an afternoon as beautiful as her spring dress.

Sarah let the other kids blow out her candles. She let everyone else eat the cake and sing the songs and raise their punch in thanksgiving.

In the midst of the celebration, Sarah is still. The still point of a turning world. The still witness to a loving God.

JULY 10, 1994

THE SPIRIT OF MALIBU

PRINCESS LOUISA INLET, BRITISH COLUMBIA

Once you've been to Malibu, it doesn't take much to send you back. The smack of rain on cedar has always done it for me. One whiff and I'm 500 miles away, holding on for dear life to a place where the days are never wasted and the nights are rarely lost.

A summer place. A beautiful, lonely place. A patch of log cabins and wooden boardwalks that, by all rights, should have surrendered to wet skies and dry rot years ago.

But God, who has a passion for long-term commitments, had other plans.

In early June, almost 40 years after the Malibu Club was born again as a meeting ground for high-school kids and Jesus Christ, the property welcomed back 120 of the cooks, boat drivers and garbage haulers who staffed the camp over the years.

We returned to the place where, more than any we'd ever known, we'd seen people brought to their knees, to the cross or to the infinitely consoling understanding that they were part of something that endured.

A club that didn't turn anyone away. A regiment where the only marching orders were to seek justice, love kindness and walk humbly with your God.

For all I know, this may be your typical summer camp experience. Friends who reached out to steady me whenever I was overwhelmed by that rain-soaked cedar have suggested as much, and they may be right.

There are, I hope, other camps where the message is so powerful that lives are transformed. Where bruising floor-hockey games, moonlight swims, midnight prayers and raucous skits are part of the program.

Where you leave your mark not by carving your initials in the toilet stall, but by running the distance, then handing the baton to someone who shares your vision, your faith, your sense of place.

Over the past 40 years, thousands of young people from Oregon have ventured to Malibu. More than 350 kids from 15 Portland-area high schools are cruising up there this summer alone.

Craig Berkman, a Republican candidate for governor of Oregon, met his wife, Susan, at Malibu. Bob Farrell, the entrepreneur behind Farrell's ice cream parlors and restaurants such as Stanford's and Newport Bay, has made the trek. So have Sen. Mark Hatfield, R-Ore.; KATU (2) anchor Julie Emry; and author/illustrators Doris Sanford and Graci Evans.

And so have legions of tender kids who were promised a great week and returned with a simple promise.

• • •

When we first set foot on this sacred ground, back in the '60s and '70s, we were traveling light. Aside from the rain gear, our only baggage was hopes and dreams.

There we were, in our early 20s, and we were spending the summer at Malibu, a Young Life club 100 miles north of Vancouver, British Columbia.

We had it made. We had the run of the place.

We had, someone once said, stepped through the wardrobe into Narnia.

Narnia, for those who have never made the trip, is the setting for seven ageless children's stories by C.S. Lewis. Even Narnia's most faithful tourists can't imagine that it is a more beautiful escape than Malibu.

The club sits on the rocks where two inlets—Jervis and Princess Louisa—meet in a torrent of rapids. In the mid-'70s, pods of killer whales would surf the rapids, chasing the seals that grew fat and lazy dining on the salmon that spawned at the head of the Jervis.

The whales have not returned in recent years—neither have many of the salmon—but bald eagles, geese and marbled murrelet still sail in the shadow of the 2,500-foot peaks that guard the inlet: Alfred, Albert and a rocky ridge of high cheekbones and jagged eyebrows that resembles the face of Frankenstein turned mournfully skyward.

The man who invaded this wilderness and put Malibu on the map was Tom Hamilton, a Seattle boy who struck it rich in the 1930s with the variable-pitch propeller and a nifty sales mission.

Hamilton was United Aircraft's European sales rep and earned a hefty commission selling Hermann Goering the engines and parts he needed to rebuild the German air force.

With more dollars than he knew what to do with, Hamilton built Malibu in the mid-'40s to celebrate his ego and lure his Los Angeles-area friends up into the Great Green North. When those friends realized that the sun didn't shine on this Malibu as it did on its Southern California namesake, they checked out, never to return.

In 1950, Hamilton followed their lead. He left so abruptly that he abandoned several yachts at the inner dock, vessels that were crushed by the winter freeze and dragged to the bottom of the inlet by the spring thaw.

Two years later, Jim Rayburn came roaring up the Jervis, in hot pursuit of another camp for Young Life, his nondenominational, Texas-based ministry.

Rayburn had several simple theories about introducing high-school kids to the Gospel. Because he had no faith in kids attending church, Rayburn loaded up on the Good News and trooped off to where the kids did hang out: the football field, the drive-in or the pool hall.

And he was a big fan of summer getaways: Lure kids out of their comfort zone and into the unknown, invite them to try something new—be it sailing, water skiing or a frantic dive down the zip line—and you might, Rayburn figured, tempt them to take their first thoughtful walk with Jesus.

Better yet, ferry them to Malibu, just about the prettiest place in all creation, and ask them to consider the Creator.

Young Life bought the Malibu Club for a mere $300,000, and in July 1954 the remodeled resort welcomed its first weekly camp: seven slightly overwhelmed girls.

Attendance would pick up. Malibu was soon host to as many as 250 kids each week, at least 80 percent of them from Young Life clubs in Oregon and Washington. Before long the camp began to show the strain.

Hamilton built Malibu to impress, not to endure. Forty miles from the nearest grocery store, the club was sustained—at least in this world—by a balky power plant, a leaking waterline, a dilapidated fleet of boats and an overworked staff. Young Life couldn't afford a crew of seasoned pros.

Of the many who jammed fingers in the dike, no one had quite the impact of Vic Hookins, once an underwater demolition expert with the British navy.

Hookins, who lorded over the property from 1962 to 1972, didn't believe in the immovable object. "If you want to move something, blast it," he said. "We don't need a discussion." Boulders, old boats, sewer lines, logjams, it didn't much matter. Hookins was a guy loaded, quite literally, for bear.

Witness the black bear that wandered down into camp one evening, scavenging for food, when Hookins was feeling a little feisty. Hookins dropped the bear with a shot to the head, then wondered how to get rid of the carcass.

Because old habits die a lot harder than black bears, Hookins fitted the beast with six sticks of dynamite, then nudged it out into the rapids. The current carried the giant furball around to the other side of Malibu where, smack in the middle of one of the evening "club" talks on sin and salvation, it lighted up the night sky.

Such disruptions were commonplace. In those days, Malibu's property and mission staffs simply weren't in sync. The garbage the kitchen staff sent out with the morning tide often returned just as the camp speaker invited kids to go sit by the water and consider the words of John the Baptist.

That all changed with the arrival, in 1972, of a bottom-line businessman named Mike Sheridan.

Sheridan inherited the management of a property that was falling apart—twice a week, on average, the waterline broke, cutting off Malibu's water supply—and put it back together.

He insisted, first off, on standards of excellence that Malibu had never known. He wanted kids who disembarked each Wednesday, exhausted by the eight-hour boat ride from Vancouver, to feel as if they'd just arrived at Disneyland.

Sheridan wanted the property to sparkle, the food to captivate and the boats to run on time. He insisted that Malibu live within its means, so he abandoned the "Fantasyland" projects, such as the ski lift up to one of the mountaintops, that were driving Malibu bankrupt.

And Sheridan did one thing more. Every dollar of capital, he decided, had to be reinvested in the physical property. That meant Malibu had to depend on volunteer labor to keep the camp running.

"I rolled the dice," Sheridan said of his crew 20 or so years ago. He entrusted Malibu's daily operation to a bunch of raw, reckless kids in their 20s who wanted more out of their summer break than a French-fry smock at McDonald's.

The Summer Staff.

The gang that broke one of Sheridan's cardinal safety rules at last month's reunion, when it climbed atop chairs in the Malibu dining room and, seizing a scene from *Dead Poets Society,* saluted the man with Walt Whitman's chorus of "O Captain, My Captain."

• • •

The laughter wasn't hard to figure. We brought our scrapbooks. We had photographs of the day Doug Beghtel—now a photographer with *The Oregonian*—and Dave Carlson, two Portlanders who worked at Malibu in the late '70s, went chasing ducks in the Ski Nautiques and discovered how stupid ducks really are.

We had the highlight of Malibu's pyrotechnic decade, the tale of the day actor John Wayne fired off a small cannon as he sailed his yacht, *The Wild Goose,* through the rapids and Vic Hookins deemed it an act of war.

While Wayne slept that night down by Chatterbox Falls, Hookins drifted quietly down with his oxyacetylene cannon and, just off the *Goose*'s bow, set off a bang that echoed in the Duke's ears for the next month.

And we had the story from head cook Gordy Sloan about the morning the tub of scrambled eggs—65 dozen in all—got knocked onto the kitchen floor five minutes before the camp stumbled in for breakfast.

Standing ankle deep in the yellow yuck, Sloan made a command decision: "There's nothing on that floor that a little heat won't kill." Up came the eggs, scooped up by six metal dust pans.

"What they don't know," the head cooks always preached, "won't hurt them."

No, the laughter was inevitable, and so were the tears.

Not every trip back to the real world—back through the wardrobe—had been kind. Over the past 20 years, not every marriage had survived. On the second night, when our reunion group gathered at the heart of camp, Kurt Stephan of Wenatchee rose and talked about seeing Christ with both eyes, one focused on the power of the Resurrection, one intent on the pain of the cross.

If one eye wanders, Stephan said, you may go blind when the doorbell rings one night and the stranger at the door tells you that your 10-year-old son is dead.

"The cross can be very dark," Stephan said. "There are things broken there that do not mend. Things that do not heal."

As Beghtel, Malibu's camp photographer in the late '70s, put it, "We are no longer bulletproof." Our baggage is heavier. We are now part of things that won't endure and deeply committed to people who don't understand why the smell of wet cedar brings tears to our eyes.

How strange, then, that most of the cries that echoed across the Princess Louisa last month were filled with the relief of what we'd found and not the pain of what we'd lost.

On our last afternoon at Malibu, a group of us sat down with Mike and Joan Sheridan, who wanted to tell us what had happened to the three kids they once brought up the inlet each summer.

Good things, mostly, and Joan wanted us to know why. Years ago, her daughter, Kim, came home one afternoon rather depressed that most of her friends had chosen to go to a place called the Smoke Hole, one of those after-school hangouts that scare parents to death.

"Why didn't you go to the Smoke Hole?" Joan asked.

"Because," Kim said, "I know another side of life."

"And you," Joan Sheridan said, gathering 40 of us into her arms with a voice that trembled with gratitude, "were that other side of life."

Malibu shaped and transformed us. When we worked on summer staff, we not only felt inexorably connected to our God but to three dozen other college kids who could finish the prayers we started.

And if we did our jobs, lives changed. Because while we were doing our jobs—whether we were pouring cement pilings, raking sand traps or loading kitchen scraps onto the tin "Pig" for the voyage to the garbage dump—others were working to persuade that week's camp of children that only one thing fit snugly into the God-sized hole inside each one of them.

"Preach Christ," St. Francis said, "and, if necessary, use words." Most of us never said a word, or a word that we remembered; we were simply planks in the platform on which the Gospel was presented. The tighter we were as a group, the fewer the kids who fell through the cracks.

And if we screwed up? Somehow our mistakes, our recklessness, the duck chases and the exploding bears, disappeared in the merciful, abiding love of God. The tide that took our garbage out brought back water pure enough to drink.

"You don't leave here with a full heart," Mike Sheridan said. "You leave behind a huge piece of yourself." But as we were once delivered to the edge of the Princess Louisa, we were blessed to go back and see how Malibu used that piece to shore up its sacred ground.

We were blessed to realize that when our daughters and sons grow too old for Narnia, they will have another place to go.

A summer place. A beautiful, spirit-filled place.

OCTOBER 11, 1994

IF IT'S TIME FOR MORTAL KOMBAT, THE TROOPS ARE HOT TO TROT

SALEM

The kids and I got our signals crossed Friday.

I had us pegged for the parking lot at Wal-Mart. They thought they'd died and gone to heaven.

You could understand the confusion. A few minutes after 5:00, we passed beneath the rubber chin of a giant inflated Donkey Kong staring out over Commercial Street, and disappeared into the divine madness of PowerFest '94.

PowerFest is the Nintendo national championship; or rather, a marketing campaign disguised as a championship. Every weekend, four tractor trailer rigs pull into four innocent hamlets, hit the air brakes and morph—that's right, morph—into a video-game valhalla.

For the rest of the weekend, kids can Nintendo out on 40 different video screens and, if they are truly obsessed, qualify for the championship next month in San Diego.

Last weekend, the purple PowerFest rig reached Salem. Brian Ray, the coordinator of this tour, has already visited 32 states and buried one rental car, but he looked quite at home in Wal-Mart's shadow.

Nintendo targets large sprawling stores unadorned by those annoying little specialty shops. At Wal-Mart, Ray explained, "I know exactly what to expect."

Thirty-cent Cokes. Jurassic Park sleeping bags. Cranberry-spice scented potholders in the Halloween display. *The Lion King* Battery-Powered Toothbrush and Stand.

And a lot of parents who, afraid their little kids might get hit by one of those falling prices, love to leave 'em outside at the video-game corral.

The trailer had 12 screens on each of its flanks, but the heart of the operation was the belly of the beast. In the cool, dark, Velcroed interior of the truck, you got tangled up in the sound of a dozen different games—Super Mario Kart, Maximum Carnage, and Charles Barkley's Shut Up and Jam—and just as many energetic kids.

One minute, you felt as if you were trapped in a rest room with a dozen hand dryers blaring; the next was a day at the beach, listening to the gulls tear into a dead starfish.

Still, it wasn't the sounds that impressed me as much as the convulsion alert.

"Warning," it said in indelible italics at the base of each screen, "Consult your physician (1) before playing video games if you have an epileptic condition or (2) if you experience any of the following while playing video games: altered vision, muscle twitching, other involuntary movements, loss of awareness of your surroundings, mental confusion and/or convulsions."

My daughters, who are 7 and 4, were as intrigued by Simba's and Nalla's toothbrushes as by any of the games they saw inside the truck. Not so my 9-year-old, Michael, and his buddy, Adam. Every time they wandered off, I knew where to find them: Hooked up intravenously to Mortal Kombat II.

I first realized this game was rubbing off on my son when, to fend off a hug, he spun 360 degrees and kicked me in the kneecap.

In Mortal Kombat II, two street fighters beat the crap out of one another. Because we won't let these thugs in the house, I was surprised my son is on speaking terms with Baraka, Reptile and the rest of the cast.

"How do you know who all these guys are?" I asked.

Michael looked both pained and disappointed. "They have names, Dad," he said.

Not to mention blood codes and killing strokes.

When it's time to administer the coup de grace, Kung Lao removes his hat and cuts his victim in half. Reptile takes off his mask and unleashes acid spit. "And Shang Tsung," Michael explained, "can morph into any of these other people."

He paused, his suspicions aroused. "Do you know what morph is?" he asked.

Of course, I do, I assured him. I use the word all the time.

Help me out here, I asked Brian Ray as a crescent moon rose over

Donkey Kong's shoulder: Are these games, or are they not, the end of western civilization?

Ray mulled it over; none of his muscles twitched. "When I was 9, I was catching Army men on fire," he said. "I hadn't been introduced to software. When these kids get involved in computers, it's a step in the right direction. I had to read about this stuff; these kids are already fluent."

Already conditioned. Already trained. They've seen blood fly on a computer screen; they know all the killing strokes.

And when it comes their turn to push a button and catch some Army men on fire, two or three Iraqi excursions down the road, they'll be kombat ready.

NOVEMBER 24, 1994

WHY WOULD YOU –
HOW COULD YOU –
LET GO OF YOUR CHILD'S HAND?

WASHINGTON

If you stepped from the freight car holding your son's hand, you joined him in the showers. That was almost automatic. The kids went to the gas chambers first. If your fingers were entwined in your daughter's, you went along for the ride. The Nazis at Auschwitz or Treblinka didn't have time to pry you apart.

The kinder guards working the railroad platforms would whisper, "Give away your baby," but what parent could heed that advice? They'd ferried the child that far. They'd kept their sons and daughters safe and reasonably well-fed in the ghetto and through the long, brutal haul of deportation.

Why would they, how could they, let go of that hand now?

It is early morning, and I am keeping a wary eye on my son, Michael. We have come to the Holocaust Memorial Museum, just a block from the Washington Monument, and I don't know if he is ready for what we will see.

I'd also wanted to bring my 7-year-old daughter, Christina, but Mary Morrison, the museum's press liaison, told me she was just too young. "We don't recommend the exhibition for children under the age of 11," she said. "But if he's a mature 9 1/2 . . ."

Michael? Mature? How do I measure that? He's not old enough to go to 7-Eleven alone on his bike. He knows the NBA better than I do, but he's not ready for *Schindler's List*.

Maybe I just want him with me. Four-foot high walls guard the view of some of the worst displays—the medical experiments and the films taken of the bodies and the bulldozers when the death camps were "liberated." Maybe I trust that I can choose what Michael sees and what he doesn't.

The museum doesn't give us much time to get ready. There is no warm-up lap. When the elevator takes you up to the fourth floor—the beginning of the long, slow descent into hell—and the doors open, you are met by a huge photograph from the concentration camp at Ohrdruf, Germany.

It is April 1945, and the American soldiers have arrived. They are staring at a funeral pyre in which the burnt branches and blackened corpses are stacked like Lincoln Logs.

Dwight Eisenhower was at Orhdruf. "The things I saw beggar description," he said. Neither do I know what to say as I turn to Michael. "Do you know what that is?" I ask.

His hands are in his pockets, his eyes on the floor. "Yeah," he tells me, and we move on. I won't know for another two hours that the image is still burning inside him.

As we follow the exhibits marking the rise of the Nazis, and the fall of the Jews, his questions come. Are the concentration camp uniforms real? Why are they burning books? How did they hang all the photographs high overhead in the Tower of Faces? Why didn't we bomb Auschwitz?

Some questions I can answer, some I can't. Maybe it's because Michael is with me, but I am pulled along by the pictures and stories of children. They stare into the cameras as if they are weapons. They are at the front of the line in Mieczyslaw Stobierski's model of Crematorium II at Auschwitz. Dr. Josef Mengele, I am told, did some of his best work on kids.

Here is a photograph of a "mentally disabled" girl at the asylum in Sonnenstein. She is 9, maybe 9 1/2 , and she is naked. Her eyes are closed in pain; at her throat, keeping her face turned toward the camera, are the fists of the nurse whose face we cannot see.

As the Nazis developed their mass-killing machines, they tested the gas and the ovens on the handicapped. This child was gone by 1941.

As our descent continues, I sometimes lose track of my son. I am too involved to follow his retreat. Now and then, I turn and see Michael in the distance, framed in the doorway of the reconstructed Auschwitz barrack. Then he returns, seeking shelter. I feel his head against my back as, peering over the 4-foot high wall, I watch the firing squads send fresh bodies tumbling into mass graves.

He is in more of a hurry than I am. I suspect that he's rushing to get to the Wexner Learning Center at the exhibition's end so he can play with the computers. But when we're seated at a work station with our headphones on, I feel him wince each time I touch the screen to call up another subject.

"No photos," he begs me. "There may be photos I don't like. That's why I don't want to stay."

And we don't. Outside, the noon sun is so bright that it hurts our eyes. The wind is sharp and cold, and Michael is fishing for lunch. Can we stop for a bag of chips? When am I going to let him ride to 7-Eleven on his bike?

Riding on the Washington subway, he asks me which goes faster, Metro or MAX back home. We talk. We argue. He leans his head against my shoulder.

I hold his hand.

A FAMILY HOME FOR THE HOLIDAYS
IS FILLED WITH MYSTERY...
AND LOVE

POTOMAC, MD.

Family is supposed to provide such certainty, but it remains a mystery. It doesn't always follow you home for the holidays. You can't leave all of the awkward, bulky baggage on the airport carousel.

We flew east last week to spend Thanksgiving with my in-laws. I know that sounds like trouble. The very word—in-laws—sounds like the broken marriage of "inmates" and "outlaws."

I prefer my daughter Christina's view of these visits. She is convinced that the song, "Over the river and through the wood to grandmother's house we go," was written and illustrated with her—and us—in mind.

Over the river and through the wood, there is a Sunday buffet laced with the aroma of fresh mozzarella, sweet peppers and Italian salami. There is a marvelous house red, one of those estate wine-bottle openers that removes the cork for you, and several brothers-in-law hooting in the background because it took me three years to figure out which way to pull the handle so that the screw grabbed the cork instead of driving it down into the bottle.

There are traditions. On Friday night, the last of the five Natelli children was married at the altar of Our Lady of Mercy. Waiting for him there was the Rev. Robert Lennon, who also married my wife Nancy's parents 38 years ago.

"I always prayed that God would let me live long enough to marry all five of these kids," Father Lennon said from the pulpit, glancing nervously at the Almighty.

In the Natelli home, you not only root for Washington's football team but you're allowed to call them by name. You vote Republican (thank God for the secret ballot). You shake your head at how Frank Sinatra's voice has held together through the years, and harmonize with it whenever possible. I still remember the night, back when Uncle Joe and Grandpa Natelli still were alive, when everyone crowded around the kitchen table and spent two hours singing Broadway show tunes and the greatest hits of the '40s and '50s.

You linger extra long with your coffee after the dinner dishes are cleared away. You kiss all your sisters-in-law goodbye even when you know you're going to see them the following morning. You find yourself singing, "Fly me to the moon..." in an empty hallway because the harmony at a kitchen table is locked inside you forever.

Each time I glance at my children, I hope they remember, remember it all. The deer that glide across the front lawn. The fireflies they trapped in a bottle. The bumpy rides in Grandpa's golf cart. The laughter they heard in the distance.

When I was a kid, my mother's parents had a house like this one in Jenkintown, on the northern tip of Philadelphia. Perhaps I feel so at home here because this is what I remember of those distant holidays. Cousins everywhere. Strangers bearing gifts. Once-a-year desserts. Aunts and uncles who seemed to love me out of all proportion to what I'd ever done for them

Dear Aunt Flora:

Thank you for the Chip Hilton book you sent me for Christmas. A Punt, A Pass, and a Prayer *is my all-time favorite. I'm sorry this thank-you letter is so late. Can you believe the Phillies are still in first place?*

What more can you say with any certainty anymore?

Some families simply bottom out. Their roots don't go deep enough to survive the droughts. You get the feeling whenever you're together that this is something that is passing, not something that will last.

That feeling doesn't haunt us here. The Natellis already have seven grand-kids and two more—none from the Oregon chapter, I hasten to add—are on the way. We are thinking of doing more with Nancy's parents, not less—

maybe Italy in the spring? Perhaps Father Lennon could watch over the kids while we're gone. You know, get to know them a little better before he meets the next generation at the altar.

On Thanksgiving Day, late in the afternoon, I sat quietly for a moment and listened. Sound carries through the house, and in the near and far, I heard the clatter of an air hockey game and the ricochet of an eight ball. The Cowboys and the Packers and Ray Charles. The shuffling of plates in the kitchen.

The voices of the past. Singing "In other words, take my hand...."

It is a mystery, the family. It is not always home when you get there. But when it is, the wind that stings the toes and bites the nose is turned away at the front door. And you are not.

DECEMBER 4, 1994

IF YOU INSIST ON KEEPING SCORE, SOMEONE MAY COUNT THE TEARS

AFTER 12 YEARS OF MARRIAGE, I'm no expert on the subject. The final draft of my column, "Surviving Marriage," isn't scheduled to run until 1997. At the very earliest.

But these are desperate times. Actor Richard Gere and model Cindy Crawford have called it quits. The blessed union of Michael Jackson and Lisa Marie Presley is rumored to be on the rocks.

I can't afford to wait any longer. Before this divorce bug gets any more contagious, I need to hustle out my rough draft.

Many of my suggestions are directed to men, which is not to suggest men have all the answers or deserve all the blame when wedlock veers toward gridlock.

Testosterone-based thinking is simply the ineptitude I'm most familiar with.

Thinking too much, or too hard, is often a problem. I yield to e.e. cummings, who once supposed:

the best gesture of my brain is less than
your eyelids' flutter which says
we are for each other . . .

For those moments when you fear that you aren't, may I suggest:

The 180-degree shift, an exercise when one aspect of your spouse's otherwise charming personality begins to gnaw on you.

If she's a party animal and you can't handle the pace, imagine her as a couch-potato recluse. If he wears his passions on his sleeve, consider the consequences of being tied to a guy whose heart has never seen the light of day.

When you complain that your mate doesn't understand you near enough, imagine being joined to someone who understood you all too well.

Toying with such potential disasters may help you to remember the initial attraction.

A lot of crucial dates belong on your calendar, but there is no future in cracks such as, "Is this the one or two-month anniversary of the last time you ironed one of my shirts?"

If you insist on picking up a copy of that delightful anthology, *Women Write Erotica,* and ask that it be gift-wrapped for Christmas, make sure you smuggle the book into the right stocking.

Yours. Not hers.

Don't keep score. Beyond the impulse to count your blessings, shelve the statistics. Don't keep track of who has the most apologies. *People* magazine cover appearances. Control of the remote control. Or who usually makes the trip upstairs to wrestle with nightmares in the middle of the night.

Ignore all the evidence that leads you to believe you are doing more than your fair share. As Billie Jean King once said, "Marriage isn't a 50-50 proposition very often. It's more like 100-0 one moment and 0-100 the next."

Employ your children as peacemakers, or angels of mercy, never as prisoners-of-war.

Demythologize the fantasy you married. Sure, she promised you everything, but who can blame her for changing her mind. She had stars in her eyes; now, she has your gut in her bed.

When heading off on boys-night-out to see Elle Macpherson in *Sirens,* first leave a note on your wife's pillow explaining that from the opening scene through the closing credits, you'll be thinking only of her.

On the rare occasion when you stumble upon part of the formula for a workable marriage, write it down. And park it where you can get your hands on it in a hurry.

Nothing fails quite so often as memory. You'd be amazed how often you revisit the same battlegrounds because you've forgotten the terms of the peace you made on your last visit.

Err on the side of more showers.

Although you're vying for permanence, bear in mind that the everlasting fabric is a patchwork of phases and moods.

Once you've repeated your vows, don't cast anything in stone. Never try to sum up your frustration in a single sentence. Don't mistake a hazardous weekend for the harbinger of a lifetime of misery.

When one stretch of the temporary gets a little rough, turn, turn, turn. This too shall pass.

An occasional review of 1 Corinthians 13 never hurt anybody.

Neither did the counsel of the Talmud, in which husbands are warned not to make their wives cry. For God counts her tears.

FEBRUARY 14, 1995

LIVING ON A HILL–
AND LIVING IT TO THE HILT–
THANKS TO THE SNOW

W E LIVE ON A HILL. And given the snow, that is all you need to know.

A snowfall such as this quickly divides Oregonians into two camps: Those who dig out their cars and those who reach for their sleds.

The dividing line is often the incline of their property.

Most of the folks who grab a shovel and chains must work at television stations. They were in our face all day Sunday, announcing freeway closures and identifying slick spots.

Those reporters shivering on overpasses did what television does so well, which is to get it all wrong. They viewed the snow as the barrier between us and where we need to go, not a blessing that keeps us home.

This was the metro area's sweetest snowfall in 25 years, and TV was obsessing on road conditions. On Monday, KATU (2) was even taking on-air phone whines about problem drivers, another landmark in our culture of complaint.

Most kids, especially those who live on hills, weren't watching television Monday. They were rolling out the sleds.

Our house is actually at the foot of one hill and tucked into the long cool arc of another. In this Lake Oswego neighborhood, the ideal sleigh ride begins in the court at the top of the first hill. If you can take the corner in front of our house, the best part of the ride is dead ahead.

If you can't, you're better off making snow angels.

Lauren—my snow angel—and I were up the hill before 10 o'clock, dragging our sled behind us.

That sled is, technically speaking, a "snow racer." The rider sits on a seat above two runners and grips a steering wheel that is attached to a third runner at the front of the sled.

Brakes? In a perfect world, you stomp your feet down on a hinge of serrated metal that sinks its teeth into the snow and ice.

A perfect world hasn't been built, however, that can accommodate a 4-year-old. With Lauren sitting in front of me, I couldn't reach the brakes.

On the morning's first ride, we discovered that the snow, though too dry for snowballs, was ideal for downhill racing.

The snow that had been packed down by passing cars had crusted into ice; the rest of the powder was like sawdust on a glass table.

Twenty seconds down the chute, and our mailbox already in the rearview mirror, the needle on our speedometer surged past 20 mph. Bouncing up and over tire ruts, we were a runaway bobsled, with the emphasis on bob.

That got me thinking, at long last, about stopping.

It was already too late to throw Lauren overboard, so I reviewed my options. Not far ahead was the front grille of a snowbound BMW. Beyond that was more hill, and not a runaway truck turnoff in sight.

The only way out was to dig my heels into the ice and steer for the nearest snowbank, the backwash of a long-gone snowplow. Oddly enough, that did the trick. When we tumbled off the sled, I kept a good grip on Lauren to ensure that she broke my fall.

She was still laughing when I brushed the powder from her face. She knew the old man had everything under control.

After several more rides, each quicker than the last, I reached for the red recycling bin and began to pack the snow-blocks for the fort in our front yard. By that time, almost 20 kids were on the hill. Half had snow racers; the rest had been advised by Mom or Dad to borrow one from the neighbors. When that failed, the ice was slick enough to bring the best out of a plastic garbage-can lid.

Now and then, a car would pass, often sideways. At the wheel was someone convinced they needed to be somewhere else, who didn't see in the snow the chance to cut the chains to their car and add a few links to their kids.

Or someone, most likely, who has a real job.

The crowd on the hill didn't thin out until early afternoon, by which time the snow fort was three blocks high. Most of the sledders were giddy, realizing no school bus would conquer this climb on Tuesday morning. Again and again, they plunged down the slope, too reckless to be scared, too happy to be cold.

By lunch time, there were a few minor injuries. Randy Sorenson bruised his leg and Christopher Haas got a small cut above the eye. Because there were a lot more kids than course marshals, several kids took flight. Tony Williams wandered off twice. After tracking him down twice to escort him home, I made him promise to phone me if he got grounded for life.

"No," he called to say, "just for today."

Tony missed the afternoon of a pretty good day. We live on a hill and on Monday, we lived it to the hilt. Given the snow, that is all you need to know.

APRIL 16, 1995

WHAT YOU HEAR
IS THE VOICE OF ANGELS

LAST SUNDAY—MASTERS' SUNDAY—I was parked on the couch, cheering on the usual suspects, the Wake Forest golfers. Lauren, who turns 5 next month, was sidesaddle in my lap, riding each bounce and wince.

We were on the back nine with Jay Haas when I asked for her help. "Say 'Get in the hole, Jay,' " I begged her. When her voice wasn't enough to drain the putt, Lauren felt my disappointment ripple through us, and turned her face to mine.

"It's OK, Daddy," she said. "You still have me."

One Sunday later, I still do, which leaves me—on this weekend of resurrection and life—especially mindful of the parents who don't.

Steve and Colleen Doell. Charles and Jeri Boley. Don and Chris McClave.

Each time a child disappears from a beach or an unguarded bedroom, or dies in the rain or the snow, she leaves behind a grief that I can't pretend to understand.

Or pretend I could overcome.

Some families never mend. The casket closes, but the wound doesn't. In the 30 months since his daughter, Lisa Marie, was willfully run down on a Lake Oswego street, Steve Doell hasn't buried his restlessness or his rage.

He haunts the state Capitol, lobbying for tougher crime laws, easy prey for any reporter looking for a victim. Whatever froze inside him when Lisa Marie died has not begun to thaw.

We warm to mercy at different speeds. The Boleys didn't come in from the cold for several years after their son, Brian, was killed by a drunken driver named Ruben Gonzalez Carillo. As the case staggered through the system, they were increasingly desperate for justice.

But when Circuit Judge Patrick Gilroy passed sentence on Gonzalez in January, imposing the maximum penalty, something changed in the Boleys. Just before Gonzalez was turned over to the Department of Corrections, passed beyond the reach of forgiveness, Charles Boley called Gilroy's office.

Gilroy still isn't sure why he took the call; he expected anger and vengeance. What he heard was the voice of the angels: The Boleys wanted Gonzalez released so he could be with his own son, Bryan, a 5-year-old dying of a congenital heart defect.

"The more important your loss is, the more invested you are in it, and the harder it is to forgive," Jeri Boley said Thursday. But forgiveness "is an act of faith. When I went up to him after the judge sentenced him and told him I forgave him, it blew him away. It also released something in him."

It released something in everyone. "I wish other parents could witness that, the release they felt," said Gilroy, a father of seven. "The goodness that came out of this horrible, monstrous event...I've never experienced that, before or since.

"I have advised others not to let the tragedy that has taken their son or loved one take the rest of their family with it," Gilroy said. "You can become obsessed. You somehow have to let go in some way and get on with your life.

"I'm sure the child that loved us would want us to move on and not let his death destroy our lives."

Some parents choose to move on, others choose to stop moving. C.S. Lewis once said that every choice we make turns us into a more heavenly creature or a more hellish one. When a child dies, it is small wonder that some parents hurled into the depths choose to conform to the scenery.

Others choose to transform it. "At some point, you have to come to grips with what is," said Don McClave, whose daughter, Susan, died on Mt. Hood nine years ago. "I'm a big believer in the notion that 90 percent of what happens to you in life you can't control. But you can sure control what you do with it."

You usually feel, the Boleys and McClaves said, as if you are on your own. Husbands and wives struggle to comfort one another because the child filled different cracks in each of their lives. They are rocked at different times by the pain.

I don't know if grace finally intervenes with or without an invitation, whispering that letting go of your anger and bitterness is not the same as letting go of your child.

"The child," Don McClave said, "is with you every day of your life. She never goes away."

And she doesn't seek to hold you back. If she can no longer heal you by turning her flawless face to yours and whispering, "You still have me," she can lay your name at the feet of the one who long ago put death in its place.

PLAY BALL:
THAT'S AN ORDER,
NOT AN INVITATION

CALL ME UNPATRIOTIC, but I got no time for this holiday. Not when it blows a four-day wide hole in my Little League schedule.

You can have your barbecues and your pool parties and your flags at half-staff. I got a schedule to keep. I got a dozen 9-year-olds who still can't turn the double play or pull off a foolproof suicide squeeze.

If you think they've got more important things to do, that's easily explained:

I'm the coach, and you're not. You're one of those moms or dads who drops their kids off at practice and never looks back.

You've got no idea whether I'm teaching them right or teaching them wrong. Driving 'em hard or giving 'em a phony pat on the back when they strike out without once swinging the bat.

Lucky for you, I know what I'm doing.

At this age, the kids sure don't. They're soft. Their minds wander. Left on their own, they wouldn't spend three hours a night in the batting cage at Malibu Grand Prix. They'd stop pitching when their throwing arm begins to ache. They don't know what they want.

Call me omniscient, but we coaches do. We know who's on first and what's on second. Because we've read Tom Boswell, we know life imitates the World Series.

And when it comes to Little League, we're the game.

It took me awhile to figure this out. I used to think teams from Beaverton and Hazel Dell always were in the winners' circle of youth baseball because they had an incredible run of home-grown talent.

But I was at the Little League park one night. There were runners on second and third when a kid laid down a nifty little bunt. The third-baseman fielded the ball cleanly enough, but he had no play on the runner at home, so he threw to first.

That runner on second? He cut third. Cut the corner. Halfway between the bases, he turned toward home. Missed tagging the bag by a mere 20 feet. This being Little League, only two umpires were on the field and both had their backs turned.

The runner beat the relay from first without a slide. Scored from second on a bunt.

It sunk in after awhile. No kid pulls a stunt like that on his own. Kids don't have the guts or the smarts. Kids don't lean into the inside pitch to get out of a slump on sheer instinct. Kids who bat right-handed don't switch over to the left side of the plate so they can block the catcher's view of the runner on first and give him a better jump on the steal.

That's where the coaches come in. At this level, the coaches are the difference. The coaches teach you all the little tricks to gain that unfair advantage.

Only the coaches know enough to teach their catchers to slap a sliding runner with a hard tag to the face. Nine-year-olds, they don't know yet that 9-year-olds can't take a punch.

Call me repetitive, but the coaches are the game. And leaving your kid to some other coach—some slob who preaches "love of the game" and allows his players to leave the dugout for the water fountain—is like leaving your kid to chance.

Not me. I'm not into child abandonment. That's why I'm in the coaching box, meeting my kid at the foul line as he comes off the field, running down the list of his mistakes while they're still fresh in his mind.

I'm hardest on my kid, of course. Got to be. If I cut my own some slack, the rest of the little buggers might think they could get away with something.

That's why I scream at him a little louder than the rest. Drag him along when I go on scouting trips. Force him to watch ESPN Sunday Night Baseball, even when the Padres are on.

Push him through those hitting and fielding drills again and again and again.

Maybe that's why he screamed back at me the other day, "Which one of us is playing this game, Dad?"

"You are," I yelled back. "And that's the problem."

We're in this together, of course. I'm doing this all for him. I'm teaching him how to win. He'll learn to choke on his own time.

Time. . . . Coaches got no time for holiday weekends. Because the little woman insisted we spend a couple nights at Manzanita over Memorial Day, I went along, but I packed the equipment bag.

And while the girls searched for sand dollars, I hit grounders to my son, trying hard to ignore all his whining that the ball didn't bounce true on the dunes and that the sand was getting in his eyes.

Two hours I kept him out there. "Can we quit now, Dad?" the kid finally asked me.

"What is this 'Dad' stuff?" I growled.

"Call me coach."

JULY 2, 1995

AND SOMETIMES YOU FIND SHELTER
IN THE HOUSE NEXT DOOR

U NTIL THURSDAY, THEY LIVED NEXT DOOR, although it often seemed closer than that. The doorbell would ring in the middle of dinner or the afternoon doldrums, and the kids would scramble for the front hall.

Because the tuft of Christopher's head broke the surface of the glass pane in the top half of the door, and Sarah's did not, the kids always knew who'd come calling. One moment they were screaming hello; the next they were gone, sucked from the house, thrilled to be alive.

When Steve and Karen first moved in, back in the summer of 1989, Chris was 2, and Sarah was fresh out of the box.

Nancy and I didn't know what to expect. You never do. I once dreamed of living on the same street with my lifelong friends, but that never happens. You end up parked too far from your dearest friends and too close to some of the rest.

So you keep your guard up. When you tell your kids not to talk to strangers, you suddenly find that most of the neighborhood meets that description. Because of the rain on the roof and the daily schedule on the fridge, we tend to seek shelter indoors, not out, and it's rare when someone slips through our defenses.

Steve and Karen did. Our families were closest, of course, at the ground level. The five kids never noticed the fence between our backyards. They were always in the thick of a squirt gun skirmish, a coloring contest or a jungle safari. Fighting for a better hold on one another. Cutting each other down with reckless disregard, then patching one another up with the most unexpected tenderness.

Their parents were never quite so intricately involved. After I mentioned Chris in a column about sledding last winter, his teacher asked how he knew me.

"Oh, very well," Chris replied. "He comes over all the time to make cocktails."

When we were together at the lazy edge of a weekend, it's fair to say, Margarita often danced in our midst. But there were also Easter egg hunts, Christmas parties and days at Manzanita. There were car pools and trips to the zoo. There were all those evenings Karen found herself three eggs, two chicken breasts or one spice short of a full meal and came running down the hill.

We weren't best friends, but we were good enough. When Nancy and I looked next door, we felt blessed by some unexpected bit of luck. We didn't mind that they could see in our windows or hear our quarrels drift through the screens.

Each time it mattered, we leaned on one another. When Steve was out of town, and Karen locked herself out of the house, she knew where to come for dinner until the locksmith happened by.

When my daughter Lauren pushed that first LEGO up her nose three years ago, Karen held the flashlight for my feeble stabs at explorative surgery.

Best of all, our children were safe together, and free to trespass through one another's lives. They didn't have to call ahead. Michael was always welcome to shoot baskets in their driveway. Chris and Sarah were always free to ring the bell.

Always? Not quite. Several months ago, Steve and Karen bought a new house with a bigger backyard—and, I suspect, less interesting neighbors—on the other side of Lake Oswego.

On the last afternoon that we lived together, all of the kids were in our front yard, throwing a baseball or pawing through the going-away basket that Christina, my 8-year-old, had arranged. She'd packed candy, a Pocahontas notepad and a Beauty figurine into a cardboard box, along with a note for Chris and Sarah.

"I care about you so much," she wrote in firm, unapologetic letters. "At least you're not moving far, far away. What if you were moving to New Jersey or something? Thank you so much. You have been so nice to me."

The air was hot and still. In the distance, we could hear the song of an ice cream truck, prowling the streets of another neighborhood. No one was saying very much.

After Karen threw the final details into the back of the Explorer, she walked down the hill. There's a house for sale in our new neighborhood, she reminded us once again. And it has a pool.

We hugged goodbye, but very lightly. "Don't make me cry," Karen said. When she herded Chris and Sarah up the walk, she didn't take the chance of looking back.

As the Explorer disappeared, our kids were oddly quiet, straining for another few notes from the ice cream man, a sign that he was drawing closer and not farther away.

Nancy and I were quieter still, listening to the pages slowly turning and the silence escaping from the house next door.

HOW THE VIDEO WATCHER WAS WON
WITH BLOOD, SWEAT AND HOPE

AFTER WEEKS OF IMPASSIONED LOBBYING, Michael, my 10-year-old son, convinced me to rent the movie *Die Hard*. To be honest, he was shooting for the sequel, *Die Harder*, but my sense of continuity wouldn't allow it.

"*Die Hard*," I assured him, "is a much better movie."

I don't know what I was thinking about. Michael and I were home alone last Saturday night when I fired up the video, which pits a New York City cop, played by Bruce Willis, against a dozen heavily armed terrorists who have commandeered a Los Angeles office building.

The language, as flip as it was profane, caught me off-guard. Willis may not have introduced my son to the ultimate four-letter naughty, but he showcased its flexibility, employing the word as verb, adjective, noun and all-around conversational condiment.

"You're not listening to some of these words, are you?" I asked Michael, trying to slap some gauze over the gaping hole in my parental conscience.

Burying his head in the pillow on the couch, his classic hear-no-evil pose, Michael assured me he was not.

We watched the first half of the movie—which was long enough for the German-speaking thugs, led by Alan Rickman, to kill half a dozen people, and for Willis to begin evening the score—before it was time for Michael to head to bed.

And it was only then, after I walked him up the stairs and kissed him goodnight, that I settled back down with the remote, hopped several channels and tumbled into the final half-hour of *How the West Was Won.*

My father didn't take me to many movies when I was a kid. But when I was 9, back in 1963, he took my brother and me to that one.

It was such a grand adventure. At that age, I wasn't uninitiated to cinematic thrills; I had already survived *King Kong vs. Godzilla.* But *How the West Was Won* arrived in Cinerama, and it lifted me out of the old Garde Theater in New London, Conn., and ferried me to some places I've never forgotten.

Down the Ohio River on a raft with the luscious Carroll Baker. Into the darkness to see the "varmint" with lanky fur trapper Jimmy Stewart. Out onto the Oregon Trail with Debbie Reynolds and Robert Preston, the latter of whom desperately wanted this match to end in marriage.

"Why, for you," Preston told Reynolds in his romantic fervor, "child-bearing would come as easy as rolling off a log."

"Well, I think I'd rather roll off a log," Reynolds replied.

There was the buffalo stampede and the gunfight on the moving train. And through it all, Reynolds was singing, "Come, come, there's a wondrous land, for the hopeful heart, for the willing hand . . ."

Don't be embarrassed if you can sing along. I did for years. Long after *How the West Was Won* disappeared from the Garde, I was curled up with the movie soundtrack, a Christmas gift from my parents.

The soundtrack was all I had, of course. Hollywood had not yet spawned Hollywood Video. Movies didn't fit into a small plastic box. No amount of impassioned lobbying could prompt your dad to bring the wrong one home.

Several years ago, my brother presented me with a copy of *How the West Was Won* on video. I had never watched it, but when Michael was back on the couch, begging for popcorn, we made a deal: I'd stand for the rest of his movie if he would sit through mine.

Thirty seconds into the *How the West Was Won* overture, Michael hit me with that stirring question of his generation, "Can we fast-forward this?"

But he settled down. When Stewart carved a heart containing his initials and Baker's onto the side of a tree, he didn't hide his head in his pillow. And his questions made me wonder about the ones I must have asked my father 30 years ago.

Throughout *Die Hard*, he was fascinated by the fate of Nakatomi Plaza, the building that is destroyed before a blood-soaked Willis walks off into the sunset and the sequel.

But during *How the West Was Won*, he was puzzled by the scene in which George Peppard comes home from the Civil War to find his mother, Eve (Baker's character), buried in a fresh grave.

"Why did Eve die?" he asked.

Of loneliness? Exhaustion? A crack in that hopeful heart? I really didn't know what to say. And because the movie, and the drive to that wondrous land out west, was already lurching on, I told my son, "Just watch."

Which, I now know, is what fathers usually are forced to do. Someone hits the fast-forward button, and they watch their sons wrestle with the scenes of violence and vengeance and the stories of perseverance and hope. We wait, popcorn and heart in hand, for them to decide which makes for a better movie and which for a sweeter life.

OCTOBER 24, 1995

NO WONDER *NEVER TALK TO STRANGERS*
IS ON THE THEATER MARQUEE

ONE FATHER TO ANOTHER, he said: I need a reality check.

His 9-year-old daughter had been invited to a sleep-over. First item on the agenda: a movie at Tigard Cinemas. The host mom planned to drop the four fourth-graders off at the theater and retrieve them several hours later.

"No way," I said, one father to another. "Nine-year-olds? Are you kidding me?"

No, he'd just gotten a serious look at a chic form of child neglect.

"It happens all the time," said Brian Basham, the manager at Tigard Cinemas. "Any day you come in here, you'll see kids 12 and under unchaperoned."

On this Sunday afternoon, Basham is parked at the heart of the 11-theater complex, directing traffic, rounding up the strays and weeding the PG-aged kids out of the R-rated lines.

He's been running the show at Tigard for three months, long enough that he's no longer surprised when a minivan pulls up in front of the box office and dumps its adolescent cargo on the curb.

"The door slides open, the parent gives them a $20 bill, and it's, 'See you later,' " Basham said. "Sometimes the parents will stand there and lie to my face. They'll go to the extreme of buying a ticket, come into the theater and then duck out the back door."

The parents don't want to watch the movie. The theater is the babysitter of last resort.

The kids? They're on their own. "Even on weekends, when we go to lock up at 12:45 or 1:00 in the morning, you've got 10 to 12 kids standing outside, waiting for a ride," Basham said.

"I stay around. I let them use the phone inside. I don't want to be sitting at home wondering what happened to them."

Isn't it reassuring that someone's concerned?

In the tomes of Oregon law—if not your neighborhood theater—a parent is guilty of child neglect if he or she leaves a kid younger than 10 unattended in a place, or for a time, that "may be likely to endanger the health or welfare of such child."

The local district attorneys have better things to do than crash Tigard Cinemas and round up all the 9-year-olds on their way to a sleep-over.

But was it that long ago that Westley Allan Dodd, looking for one more child to feast upon, slipped into the New Liberty Theater in Camas, Wash., and tried to steal away with a 6-year-old boy?

"When we interviewed him, he confessed to us, 'I went to a theater because I knew there were kids there,' " recalled Lt. C. W. Jensen, the Portland Police Bureau spokesman. "Do I think he's the only one who would come up with that idea?

"No."

But a predator such as Dodd couldn't succeed again, could he? Surely, parents are more aware of the danger. Surely, theater personnel—knowing they're a dumping ground for kids while Mom and Dad go shopping at Nordstrom—are increasingly vigilant.

Basham shakes his head at such naivete: "I've been doing this for two years now. You notice different characteristics about people. Clothes, shoes. You have a pretty good feeling about who comes in with whom.

"But every weekend, we get several thousand people coming through here. The volume level gets pretty high. If someone wanted to abduct a child of a small age, I don't know if they'd be heard."

When he worked at the Washington Square Cinemas, Basham said, the baby-sitting problem was even worse owing to the proximity of the mall.

Jim Gilsdorf, the current manager at that theater, said he has a bigger problem policing the R-rated movies. When he watches a group of 13-year-olds buy tickets to *Babe*, he knows he'll spend most of the next two hours guarding the door to *Mallrats*.

But as the audience from each show filed out Sunday afternoon, 10-, 11- and 12-year-olds were left lingering at the curb, waiting for a ride home. Just inside the door, other kids played video games, enjoying the enchanting absence of adult supervision.

When three of them ran out of quarters, they quit the theater and loped off across the theater parking lot. The oldest of the trio was 12, max; the youngest no more than 5. They were in no hurry. They had no idea I was following them.

The three kids crossed six busy lanes of traffic as they cruised toward the mall; the 5-year-old looked as if he'd grown up dodging cars. They passed two Beaverton police officers arresting a guy at a bus stop as if it was nothing they hadn't seen before.

They eventually slipped into Sears. By the time, I parked the car, I'd lost them.

Whether they ended up in the aloof grip of their parents, or the loving embrace of someone else who was stalking them, I really couldn't say.

JANUARY 2, 1996

OR—PERISH THE THOUGHT—
YOU COULD DO IT YOURSELF

HOWEVER ORNERY MY HOUSE IS ACTING when my in-laws arrive, the place is subdued by the time they leave. In two or three days, Nancy's father bulldogs every stubborn problem that's stymied me for the past 18 months.

He can't abide leaving Nancy with a headache that will annoy her until his next visit. (Thank goodness I'm still on her good side.) Through the years, he has built a play table, wired in our fax, repositioned the overhead light in the kitchen and installed a shower.

Nothing slows him down. Oh, now and then he'll pause and ask what in the world I was doing for 30 years while my own father was trying to teach me to do this stuff. But then he returns to the task at hand. I keep quiet and fetch the tools, most of which he bought on his last visit or the one before that.

This Christmas, Dad serviced the fax and popped in a half-dozen dimmer switches before he got around to the desk problem.

Nancy has been looking for an affordable partners' desk for years without much luck. Dad spent 10 minutes at the tiny rattan unit that's filled in before deciding it was time for our luck to change.

Nancy's parents found the answer to our prayers, strangely enough, at Office Depot: A pair of desks that, placed back to back, gave us a flight deck of work space.

We went to see the desks the day after Christmas. They looked good. Three file drawers. That "classic cherry finish." And the price was right.

Some assembly required? You bet. According to an empathetic green card, you could call the folks at 1-800-WRTA (We're Ready to Assemble) NOW and shell out another $60. Or you could do it yourself.

"It comes in about three pieces," the salesman said. Dad had a tough time hiding his disappointment.

Office Depot promised free delivery by Wednesday afternoon, 15 hours before Nancy's parents were scheduled to fly home. A customer service manager finally showed up at 4PM with four large, flat boxes in the back of his minivan.

When we popped open the first box, we found three pieces, all right... three pieces for every man, woman and child in Southwest Portland. Dad was laughing. Me? I'm looking for that 800-number and wondering if the 60 bucks covered room and board.

"It's a shame," I finally said, "that you'll have to catch that later flight."

When the guts of the first desk were spread across the den floor, the final count was 186 parts, not counting the screws and the "hidden connectors."

Had I been alone, there's no telling how long I would have stared at the modesty panel and the pencil drawer, searching for the necessary confidence or the Phillips screwdriver.

Given that the 10 different kinds of screws were shown "actual size" on each page, I suppose the panic would have worn off eventually. But we'll never know. My father-in-law was there.

I once heard of a marriage retreat where the first question they asked of each couple was to describe the dinner hour in their home when they were growing up. The idea was to remind each spouse of the different expectations each brings to the table.

Because she grew up in her father's house, Nancy expects everything to work. Time and again she watched the annoying and the insurmountable disappear under Dad's deliberate calm, never to be seen again.

It's a rare parent who has the tools to deal with both. And who, as the problems become more complicated, adjusts his grip so that he won't be quite so necessary the next time around.

But it is that calm that I've always found the most instructive. It is a daunting yet comforting assurance that you can build it, fix it or confront it yourself.

Working side by side, Dad and I assembled the first desk in slightly less than five hours, not counting time off for the red wine and homemade vegetable soup. The second time around, we found our rhythm and cut that time in half.

And when we reached the last drawer and found ourselves one 9/16-inch large-head screw short, I scrounged through the tool box until I actually found a duplicate.

Let me tell you, Dad was impressed.

We finished up just as "Letterman" came on. Not that Dad noticed. All he'd asked for his trouble was a piece of Nancy's chocolate pudding cake. But when I went to bed, the plate was untouched, and Dad and my Phillips screwdriver were sizing up an obstinate door in the china cabinet.

When I drove Nancy's parents to the airport Thursday, the hand that gripped the wheel was blistered and red. But when I got home, a new desk was waiting for me, one I helped to build, anchoring me to the calm I need to pass on to the kids who will chip and scratch that classic cherry finish.

PASSING ON
WHAT WE DIDN'T LEARN
FROM OUR PARENTS

THE BEDROOM DOOR WAS CRACKED OPEN. That must have been it. I was 14 the night Lynn Hayhurst, who lived in the house behind ours, came by. I don't know how long we pretended to do homework before we ended up sitting on the edge of my bed, liplocked as it were.

We weren't there long before my silent alarm told me that my father was rolling down the hall. There wasn't time—or sufficient incentive—to break the clinch before his shadow passed by that telltale crack in the door.

Within a week, everything I wanted to know about sex but was afraid to see in a book landed on my desk.

A lot of Lake Oswego fifth-graders know the feeling. On Tuesday morning, they will begin three weeks of explicit but guarded instruction in what they now call human growth and HIV/AIDS.

Parents were given a chance to preview the program, even as they were offered the option of keeping their children out of it. But the 3-day weekend was their last chance to give their sons or daughters a briefing before the kids see their first official training films in the war of the sexes.

After MTV, or a steady diet of rock on NRK, you might wonder what's left to say, much less how to say it. The sex talk is no family heirloom, passed down from generation to generation. Even after Lynn Hayhurst slipped through the hedge and into my room, my parents weren't going to give me more than a sterile library book.

Their fingers were crossed, but their lips were sealed (which was just fine with me). Old habits die hard.

"When we were your age, it just wasn't discussed," my mother reminded me Sunday night. "There was nothing on television; Lucy and Desi weren't sleeping in the same bed. When Rhett swept Scarlett up the steps, I really wasn't sure what had happened up there except that she was smiling like the Cheshire cat the next day.

"We really didn't know what was going on. Nobody ever talked to me about sex. Everything I ever learned was from my friends or my sisters."

My father didn't even have that tutelage. His father died when he was 3 and his two older brothers never looked back. His mother? She worried about all the things she couldn't chaperone. On the night he graduated from high school, my dad was running late in driving his date home when he passed an angry woman on a midnight march through New Ulm, Minn.

"She was out looking for me," my father said. But when he got home, she didn't ask which hook or button had held him up. "She was mad as all heck, but there was never any discussion about what I was doing."

There are only so many options when you stay out too late with the girl of your dreams. On the night 30 years later that I pulled into my driveway at 3AM and the headlights collided with my parents, glaring like night owls at the mouth of the garage, there weren't many questions, either.

Children today come home with the answer to the question that matters the most: Are you safe? Because that it is an increasingly difficult question to answer, we hit our kids with the sex talk at age 10 instead of waiting for the playground grapevine to get sufficiently explicit.

If we don't speak to them, after all, who grabs them by the ear? Magic Johnson? Madonna? The showgirl graduates of *Saved by the Bell*?

The stakes are different. Mistakes may mean death, not unexpected life. When the don't ask-don't tell attitude about sex was finally breached in my junior high health class, the boys were dragged into one room (by the football coaches, of course) the girls into another, and never the twain did meet.

In a concession that the twain does meet, the fifth-graders in Lake Oswego will sit through the entire curriculum together except for the films that detail the initial tremors of sexual maturity. Even then, the girls and boys will watch both films.

I suspect they already know much of what's coming. Michael, my 10-year-old, certainly had a good idea why I was invading his space Sunday night, which explains why we were both giggling nervously at the start.

But we survived the 45 minutes better than I would have hoped. We haven't stopped talking yet. The door to his bedroom still is cracked open.

By the way, my father told me, "I didn't peek in your door." And if my shadow is constantly across Michael's path, I will never stoop to peek inside his door, either.

I wouldn't think of it. That's what the in-house surveillance system is for.

MARCH 12, 1996

NOT ALL OF THE DOGS
ARE HOMEWARD BOUND

M Y MISTAKE WAS STOPPING. Swerving to avoid the soggy little doormat was instinctive, but I had to think about stopping. Even then I tossed and turned and drove another quarter-mile down the road before I swung the doggone car around.

The Shih Tzu still was dodging bullets when I pulled onto the shoulder of the blind curve. She was awfully glad to see me; she came crawling on her belly across the wet gravel and glued her squished little face to the palm of my hand.

So what are ya gonna do? If you leave the dog by the road, the next Dodge that darts around the bend scrapes Shih Tzu off its license plate. But if you take her home . . .

Dog hair. Kid dementia. Divorce court.

Last Tuesday's spasm of sentimentality aside, dogs aren't us. Never had 'em, never will. We're not down on dogs; we're just not jealous of our friends who have one barking in the basement. Sorry, guys, we tell the kids each time they sit up and beg, the beast would be a burden.

All of which I patiently explained to the Shih Tzu as we drove home, the dog curled up by the heater vent below the passenger seat. She was very wet and very hungry, lapping up the Cheerios and cookies I scrounged up for her.

Because the Shih Tzu didn't have a collar or tags, I drove aimlessly around Mountain Park for an hour, looking for someone who recognized her flat face. For all the oohs and aahs, no one was willing to take the handoff.

When I brought the dog back the second time, the kids were home. My daughters named her (Corduroy), fought over her, sat with her in the dark of the garage until she fell asleep in a cardboard box, and cried the next morning as they waited for the bus.

All the while, the Shih Tzu never made a sound. She was gone by 9 o'clock Wednesday morning. The Lake Oswego animal control guy who took her out to the county pound in Oregon City was fairly upbeat. The county keeps unclaimed strays for only five days, he said, but the smaller hairballs have a good chance of being claimed or adopted.

Still, we wondered whether we'd signed her death certificate. The girls and I put up signs and knocked on more doors during the weekend, but we didn't get anywhere. The lost-and-found ads in the paper said nothing about a Shih Tzu on the lam.

On Monday morning—Day 5—I drove out to the county pound, a white cinder-block bungalow off Kaen Road. Lynn McManus was hosing down the outside runs, but she told me I could walk through the cellblock and check out the roster.

OK, so she didn't say "cellblock," but she didn't need to. Most of the 32 cells, each measuring 3 feet by 5 feet and designed for a single dog, were double-booked. There were three husky puppies in one pen, two blue tick hounds in another and a potbelly pig in a third.

And there in pen No. 14, shoulder to shoulder with a half-baked poodle with mange, was Corduroy.

She couldn't reach my hand through the chain link, but—for the first time—she raised her voice. That Shih Tzu yelp all but disappeared in the visceral panic that rolled through the pens.

Overcrowding has been a problem at the shelter since animal control officers raided Ann Hunter's West Linn compound in September 1993.

They rescued 37 cats and 20 dogs from the house. Hunter was found guilty of 37 counts of animal neglect, but when she appealed that verdict, the county was forced to keep the surviving animals locked up.

Two Ibizan hounds and 21 cats, most of them stir-crazy Orientals, still remain at the shelter 31 months later. Isn't this perpetuating their abuse?

"Absolutely," said Ross Cravens, the dog control manager, noting that the unreimbursed bill for their keep now is $94,000. "We've been converted into an old cat shelter by the legal system. We have limited space, and limited space means more dogs are put down."

Of the 2,145 animals that arrived at the pound in 1995, 967 were euthanized. The rest were adopted or claimed by their owners.

McManus, who has taken eight dogs home to her farm, says she'll sometimes keep a lap dog around for weeks, hoping someone will decide to save its life before the pound runs out of room.

On the door of Corduroy's cage hung a small red "Hold" card. On the same day the Shih Tzu arrived, someone wandered in and decided they could offer her more than the garage and a cardboard box.

By the time you read this, she will have left those huskies, the hounds and that sorry poodle behind. If their Death Row barking isn't haunting her little Shih Tzu brain, it won't soon stop echoing in mine.

APRIL 2, 1996

THE BACKGROUND MUSIC
IN OUR CHILDREN'S LIVES

As SOON AS WE GET IN THE MINIVAN, the harangue begins. My son is desperate. He wants his NRK.

If Michael has outmaneuvered his sisters for the front seat, he's reaching for the radio. If he's stuck somewhere in the back, he's lobbying long distance. He doesn't want the windows open or the windows closed. He doesn't want to know if we're almost there.

He just needs another blast of noise, another fix of the familiar, from NRK.

A year into "Portland's new rock revolution," KNRK (FM 94.7) is parked in the middle of the road in the last Arbitron ratings, drawing slightly more listeners in the 12-and-older category than KGON and significantly fewer than Z100.

But in Michael's world, and in the earphones of his friends, NRK is the only background music. NRK's playlist—chock-full of Smashing Pumpkins, Nirvana, Red Hot Chili Peppers and Alanis Morissette—is their daily nutritional supplement.

It's not that I don't understand the attraction, the power of music when it fills a room and squeezes out all the unwelcome visitors.

But my son is only 10 years old. And his acceleration into adolescence has caught me flat-footed.

When the parental slope is this treacherous, it's hard knowing where to put your foot down. Of course, I knew this cultural epiphany was coming. At 41, I still remember succumbing in my teens to Grand Funk Railroad, Strawberry Alarm Clock and the Amboy Dukes.

I can see the black-light poster I created with phosphorescent paint, carefully tracing the lyrics, "The world is a bad place, a terrible place to live, but I don't want to die," and hanging those cheerful sentiments on my bedroom wall.

And I remember feeling that every 33-rpm album was another layer of splendid isolation, a little extra breathing room between me and everyone else in the house who had no idea what I was going through.

But a generation later, this is all playing—or replaying—out too soon. Even in a world where the headlines tell me that 15-year-olds are receiving mandatory jail sentences, 12-year-olds are committing suicide, and 10-year-olds are putting guns to one another's heads, this is happening before I had any time to prepare.

Is it MTV and the seductive allure of the visuals? Is it the result of surrendering our kids time and again to the nearest electronic babysitter?

Or is it just payback?

I have no quarrel with Michael's taste in music. When NRK uncorks the Gin Blossoms' "Follow You Down" or Rancid's "Ruby Soho," I'm often singing right along. And Alanis Morissette's "Ironic"?

A traffic jam when you're already late
A no-smoking sign on your cigarette break
It's like 10,000 spoons when all you need is a knife
It's meeting the man of my dreams
And then meeting his beautiful wife
And isn't it ironic . . . don't you think?
A little too ironic . . .

It used to take four years of undergraduate English classes to explain irony, and here's Morissette serving it up on a plate.

But whenever Michael disappears into his radio or his CD player, I hear a door closing behind him. I feel him retreating to an unfiltered place where his parents are not particularly welcome.

What are you gonna do? When do you cut your kids some slack? How soon do you stop giving them spoons and hand them a knife, knowing they may take a stab at the ties that bind them to you?

Michael and I are still connected; NRK hasn't yet changed that. When he called the "My Life Sucks" request line, which rewards the best burst of self-pity, he admitted later that he struck out because he didn't have much of a sob story.

And when the two of us unexpectedly found ourselves listening on Saturday to "Detachable Penis" by King Missile, I think it was Michael who blushed first and reached for the off button.

But the following day, I was talking to him about his weekend transgressions. We were alone in the car, and when I was out of breath, we drove in silence for 30 seconds until Michael shrugged and asked, "Can I listen to the radio?"

"Go ahead," I finally said. He leaned toward the radio, its hip voice and its sympathetic ear, leaving his old man alone at the wheel, slowly chewing on the bitter root that when our kids need us the most, they're pulling away instead of drawing near.

And isn't it ironic, don't you think?

A little too ironic . . .

APRIL 14, 1996

THE TIGHTROPE AND THE SAFETY NET

OUR KIDS' LIVES INVARIABLY HANG in the balance, suspended between caution and temerity, the voice of responsibility (Mom) and the prophet of adventure (Dad) whispering in opposite ears.

In your home, those roles may be reversed; in ours, they are well-defined. My wife senses danger that I can't imagine. Hers was the gasp you heard last week when the winners of the Middle School Science Bowl were awarded plane rides from Hillsboro to Tillamook.

"They may even get to take over the planes' controls for a short time," the short story in *The Oregonian* said.

Not our kids. Not a chance. Had one of our kids been so rewarded, Nancy wouldn't have allowed her into a small plane, much less encouraged her to goose the throttle. If my wife is not averse to risk—she took quite a chance on me—she has no patience when it courts her children.

And no sympathy for my nonchalance. By nature, by faith, by virtue of the disasters that I survived, I am far too relaxed about the nightmares that may be waiting for the kids.

Because I am usually oblivious to the hot stoves, riptides and thunderstorms that trigger Nancy's silent alarm, I take the kids places they otherwise would not go.

Jurassic Park, the movie? No problem.

Jurassic Park, the park? Well, all right . . . just make sure you fasten that seat belt and keep the window rolled up.

As parents, we are forever pushing our kids out and pulling them back. We encourage them to live and beg them not to die. We struggle to hold on without holding them back.

As we whisper our fiercely conflicting messages, we strike a balance, a balance that didn't exist for Jessica Dubroff.

In home-schooling this 7-year-old, while denying her television and toys, Jessica's divorced parents, Lloyd Dubroff and Lisa Blair Hathaway, may have been doing a lot of the right things for their daughter.

But in the wake of Thursday's plane crash, which killed Jessica, her father and her flight instructor, both parents have taken a beating.

Lloyd Dubroff has been cast as a misguided, publicity-seeking fool. Lisa Blair Hathaway, facing down one television camera after another, has come across as too much of a visionary to be silenced by her grief.

"I beg of people to let children fly if they want to fly," Hathaway said. "Clearly, I want all my children to die in a state of joy. I mean, what more could I ask for? I would prefer it was not at age 7, but God, she went with her joy and her passion. Her life was in her hands."

Which, Hathaway isn't willing to concede, isn't a particularly safe place for a 7-year-old's life to be.

Dubroff and Hathaway were, apparently, intoxicated by the old Tom Robbins line, "If you want to change the world, change yourself." They just found their daughter a lot more malleable.

These architects of their child's destiny were so busy making a statement about living on the edge that neither ever paused to ask whether the risks justified the opportunity to play *Good Morning America*.

There was no check on their sense of adventure. No fear. No safety net.

Were Jessica's parents romanced by the TV cameras that went along for the ride? Were they emboldened by her blissful, childlike ignorance? Or were they just so doggone proud of their daughter's dance across the tightrope that they disdained all caution?

Her plane never got 40 feet off the ground after taking off Thursday in Cheyenne. Jessica couldn't have had time to think about what had gone wrong before the impact knocked all thought from her head.

The rest of us will continue to struggle with that each time our kids ask us if they can go to the mall or ride their bike to the park or wade out into a current we do not trust.

In other words, each time they ask us to open the door and let them fly from the cage in which we keep them, as much for our safety as theirs.

Hathaway talked to her daughter moments before the Cessna took off. And when she talked to the TV cameras, she was still enchanted that her little girl didn't fret about the approaching storm.

All Jessica said, according to her mother, was, "Do you hear the rain? Do you hear the rain?"

That's a 7-year-old for you. It's the grown-ups' job—their job and their curse—to listen for the thunder. Would that every home have at least one adult who's up to the task.

AS IT WAS IN THE BEGINNING:
A TALE OF PAIN AND JOY

GIOI, ITALY

Con dolore partiro Gioi.

Late in the afternoon of Nov. 8, 1924, when the autumn light was beginning to fade, Giuseppina Parrillo carefully scrawled those words on a plaster wall.

She was standing in a two-story stone building in the *campagna*, the family farmland. One half of the top floor was a stable; the other half a makeshift dorm room where the Parrillo children slept when, after a day of picking olives and harvesting the *melanzane*, or eggplant, they were too tired to climb the mile uphill back to Gioi.

Sickles and dried corn hung from the rafters, but there was little else in the room beside the sagging beds and the rough blankets and the sympathetic walls to which the Parrillos would turn when their worlds were falling apart.

Con dolore partiro Gioi. "With pain I am leaving Gioi."

Giuseppina was leaving home in the morning, breaking away as 7 of the 11 Parrillo children eventually would, some for Montevideo in Uruguay, the others for the United States.

She was not the first to go. Her sister, Maria, left Gioi—which is named for the Greek god, Jove, and pronounced "Joy"—three years earlier, floating down out of from the hills on her wedding day with her husband, Nicola, and heading for Naples.

The newlyweds sailed for America on borrowed money. They crossed the Atlantic in steerage, emerging briefly into the sunlight of Ellis Island, then disappearing into the wave of immigrants who found their new world in the bowels of Jersey City.

Maria and Nicola—Mary and Nicholas—began their new life in a row house, sharing a bathroom with strangers. They waited 15 years for a home of their own, with a garden for the zucchini and the tomatoes and an arbor for the grapes that Nicholas pressed into wine in his garage.

But even when he was digging ditches or working in the knitting factory, Nicholas never questioned the decision to leave Italy. He never re-crossed the Atlantic. He never returned to Gioi.

Neither did Mary or any of the other Parrillo children, save for Giuseppina, and then only long after her parents had died.

You can still see the stone skyline of Gioi perched high above a valley of dry creekbeds. The *campagna* is much quieter now—few children remain to walk the *melanzane* up the mountain at night—but in the last 70 years, little else has changed.

Old men still play cards in the middle of the narrow, twisting streets, and kids play soccer in the shadow of a 17th-century convent. The sanctuaries of Santo Eustachio and Santo Nicola are dark and cool, and if you need something from the mini-market during *mezzogiorno*, or afternoon, you need only to ring the bell of the proprietor who lives upstairs. From the top of the hill, you look down over miles of olive trees.

You can't see the farmhouse, but it is still there, guarding the cots and the dried corn and the writing on the wall. A donkey now lives in the basement with 15 hens who must wonder where all the people went.

Giuseppina went to America with tears in her eyes, as did Mary and Nicholas. They spent a lot of years without a large yard or a savings account, but they never doubted that the place they'd found offered far more than the place they'd left.

That is not to say they forgot.

Mary always urged her five children—four of whom survived—not to throw their old winter coats or blankets or tired shoes away. And when the mound of castoffs grew high enough, Mary would stuff it into a flour sack, sew up the top, carefully print the family name and address on the burlap and drag it down to the Jersey City post office.

Off it would go, bound for Gioi. If the old drapes didn't quite match the decor in the living room of the Parrillo home, they ended up as blankets on the farmhouse beds.

It would be unfair and untrue to suggest that the children of Mary and Nicholas never felt the pain that Giuseppina, their *Zia Peppina*, felt in leaving Gioi.

But they all ended up with larger yards, and they never dug ditches to keep their families fed—large families filled with Nicolettes and Francines and Antonias and other dark-skinned daughters, one of whom moved to Oregon 14 years ago and cast her lot with a sportswriter.

When we climbed up to Gioi at the end of June, she found the names of Mary and Giuseppina and the rest of the Parrillos still etched in the fading light on a plaster wall.

If Mary never returned to the top of the mountain, Mary's granddaughter did, carrying her memory up the hill and back down again.

OCTOBER 31, 1996

BUCK NAKED SUGAR

CHRISTMAS IS STILL, by the barest of margins, the best holiday, but Halloween is the most honest. The accent is on "Take." The password is "Gimme."

The enduring message of this endless night is, "I got mine, baby, and it weighs more than yours."

For both the angels and the little demons headed for your door, the hallowed heart of Halloween is not the masquerade but what's finally unmasked:

That mistletoed, silver-belled bunk about it being more blessed to give than to receive.

If you are heavy with child—any child under the age of 15—you know the raw power of Halloween.

This night was designed with kids in mind. Unlike Christmas, Halloween doesn't happen when their eyes are closed.

There may be jelly bellies in the mix, but there's no jelly-bellied middle man deciding who's been naughty and who's been nice.

And forget the sugarplums: Halloween is just plain sugar.

Buck naked sugar. All they can carry. All they can eat.

All they can bury beneath their bed, the ultimate revenge for that not-too-distant day when you scream, "You said what to your mother? Go to your room!"

And you can swear you hear, as they dash out of sight, "Don't mind if I do."

Halloween hands kids not just the candy, but also the controls. It's their turn to dress up (at my house, at least) as a witch, a spider and Ross Perot. Their turn to play in the street and dance in the dark.

Their turn to walk slowly away from a dimly lit porch, muttering, "A Tootsie Roll pop? A lousy, red Tootsie Roll pop? I'll be back in five years with a cherry bomb."

And it's a treasure hunt they don't have to share with Mom and Dad. OK, so now and then an adult tries to crash the party, answering the doorbell with a hatchet in the middle of his forehead and waiting for them to scream.

Like after they've seen Vic Atiyeh primping himself on TV for the cigarette companies, they could be scared off by some madman with an ax.

More often, parents don't count for much on this ghoulish night. We're just the valet holding the umbrella or the dumb waiters pushing the dessert tray.

They don't have to give us a cut. They don't have to write us thank-you notes.

Halloween is an early lesson in free trade: Once the kids empty their bags, they discover the fair market value of a box of Skittles.

The night reveals the sugar-coated lining of the urban growth boundary: Ten handouts per acre instead of a measly seven.

And the holiday is a reminder that some kids never grow up.

Take the Spadas. If you're a kid living near Lake Oswego High School, you know the Spadas. Cheryl and Ernie are such legends that when a "For Sale" sign recently popped up in front of their house, several neighborhood kids drafted a letter begging them to stay.

At least through Halloween.

About six years ago, the Spadas realized that few kids were taking the long walk up their driveway.

So, they started passing out 7-ounce Hershey bars.

Which, on Halloween, is the equivalent of a winning an $83 million Powerball ticket.

Word got around. About 400 kids are expected at the Spadas tonight, Cheryl reckoned, counting those on the tour buses from Hood River.

They'll all walk back down the driveway believing they've been to milk chocolate heaven.

Like kids all over town, they'll all go home and count their blessings, feeling like Uncle Scrooge in his money vault.

And long after Halloween is gone, they'll play with its ghost and chew on the memories.

RIDING A READING TIGER

THE HIGH COST OF EDUCATION JUST HIT HOME.

And you'll forgive me if I'm a little anxious to get back there: Every extra minute I spend inside this column—and outside the tent of a good reading light— is costing me money.

The financial debacle began in the last days of August when my kids were clearly floundering in the late-summer riptide of cartoons and video games.

Read a book, I suggested.

"Suck an egg," they replied.

Make you a deal, I said. Let's all keep a record of every page we read between Sept. 1 and Christmas.

And for every page you read more than I do I'll pay you...

(What's it gonna take? A penny? Naah...)

A nickel.

The kids were sprinting for the bookshelves before that nickel hit the floor. By dinner time, I was down four bucks and feeling like Shaquille ("When you learn how to read, adventures come to you") O'Neal.

We needed a day or two to establish the ground rules. Previously-read books didn't count. "What about comic books?" my 9-year-old asked.

I don't think so. Keep your own score, I said, begging the two older kids to allow the youngest, who is 6, a little artistic license with her math.

After all, I said, you're not competing against each other. You're competing against me.

(And no matter how much you read, I got you covered. Me and Stephen Hunter and James Lee Burke are gonna lap the field.)

I was pretty proud of myself. That lasted until our next trip to the library when my son, Michael, arrived at the check-out stand with 11 books by R.L. Stine.

Stine writes adolescent horror fiction. He has written two books a month for the last 25 years. Books that call "Fear Street" home. Books like *Call Waiting* ("Someone just put Karen on hold. Permanently.")

Books that go down like chocolate pudding.

There really should be a limit of books by the same author, I said.

"That wasn't one of the rules," Michael replied.

Don't you think you're defeating the purpose of this, I sniffed, nudging him out onto the guilt plank.

I can still hear him laughing.

I tried to slow him down. Took him to movies. Ordered him to 7-Eleven. I even gave him *The Little Shepherd of Kingdom Come* ("Gosh, but I loved this when I was a kid"), one of those old-fashioned books where someone doesn't get their throat slashed or their phone cord cut at the end of each chapter.

And I hustled to keep pace. Read early, read late. Read Richard Hoyt and Donald Harington, Kurt Vonnegut and E.L. Doctorow, Sandra Dallas and Turk Pipkin.

That's right, Turk Pipkin. *Fast Greens*. Golf book. Big print. Small pages.

All told, I've turned over almost 4,000 new leaves in two months...and I'm still getting smoked.

"I'm up to 4,961 pages," Michael said Thursday night.

"As of 8 o'clock," the speed-reading midget added.

His night light was still on when I went to bed.

You can do the math. I'm $50 in the hole and I'm still losing ground. The kid has already read 31 books (21 by Stine) and wants to know if I'll be paying by cash or check.

If you were a real man, I grumble, you'd wade into *Finnegan's Wake*.

He ignores me. He still has 130 R.L. Stine books in reserve. He's kicking me. I'm down. I'm almost out of options.

(Duin, please come see me about your latest expense account...)

Now, if you'll excuse me, I gotta book.

And I'm trying to remember: Do comic books count?

FEBRUARY 16, 1997

BABYSITTIN' BOOGIE

THIS IS AN ODD TIME FOR MELANCHOLY. I should be dusting off the social calendar and planning grand adventures.

At long last, my wife and I are on the verge of retiring from...the babysitter's club. We are (almost) free at last from the exhausting chore of harmonizing our weekend plans with the most forgiving young lady on the block.

If Nancy and I aren't going too far or staying too long, our son—now a solid 11—can be trusted to burrow into the couch and, through a series of grunts and hand gestures with the Nintendo control, keep the peace with his sisters while we're out on the town.

I should be celebrating. It's been a dozen years since Nancy and I could catch a matinee or a casual dinner without first conferring with half the teenagers in town.

Instead, I'm wrestling with the things I never said to the girls who held down the fort in our wake; to the two Sarahs and Heidi and Nicole; to Carley and Brita and Shawna and Katherine.

To the girls who are now on homecoming courts and college campuses. To the babysitters who accepted four bucks an hour when we were desperate enough to pay $20. To the angels who saved our marriage.

You rarely do say goodbye to a pedigree babysitter. Just when they feel like family, they disappear without a word. One minute they're watching MTV when you unlock the front door; the next they have soccer games, boyfriends or jobs at the mall.

They don't glance back. They don't call and request one more night with the kids for old time's sake. They don't miss us.

They don't know much more about us, after all, than our capacity to call at the last minute and beg.

As a result, the relationship between babysitters and parents doesn't engender many classic moments. I only have one in the file: Not that many years ago, a guy in town drove his babysitter home . . . and kept driving until they reached the beach.

You think that was a neat trick? His wife eventually forgave him.

What I usually had going with sitters was a lot of awkward conversation on the drive home. Even though all the buttons on the minivan's radio were keyed to the cool stations, they never conceded that I could possibly be tuned in to what it was like to be young (again).

I'd serve up stupid questions; they'd return blank looks. I fought the silence; they usually embraced it. After several hours with my tireless menagerie, they were tired, and I was tiresome.

What was I trying so hard to say?

That I couldn't thank them enough for allowing us to sneak out of the house. That the relief of hearing them say, "Yeah, I can do that," was no less than what Houdini felt when the straitjacket finally released him at the bottom of the pool. That I'd still remember their missions of mercy when they had babies of their own.

Not every sitter remembered to turn the oven off or the nightlights on. Not every sitter came back for more. But we had a pretty nice run: The nights we came home to find the kitchen sparkling and the dishwasher on; the father who agreed (for a six-pack of beer) to relieve his daughter when we were running late.

And then there were the moms who shook the phone tree to find a replacement when their daughters got sick at the last moment.

But what I'll remember most of all are the echoes of saying goodnight as these girls hurried to their front doors, leaving me shivering and goofy beneath the stars, hoping our children will grow up to be that decent, that spontaneous, that forgiving when some strangers call for help.

MAY 20, 1997

THERE ARE NO ATHEISTS
IN DUGOUTS

AT 8 O'CLOCK SATURDAY MORNING, the dads are out on the infield dirt with the rakes, scratching at the hardpan, softening the landing areas in front of the bases and searching out the bad hops.

The first pitch of the day's first Little League game won't roll off the mound for another hour, but the aging grounds crew is frantic to find a reason to linger on the base-paths.

They don't belong out there. The baseball diamond is no longer their turf, their proving ground. When it matters, when the game begins, the fathers must retire to the bleachers or to the metal cage of the dugout.

They must abandon the field to their sons.

On this Saturday, the fat sun and a thin breeze are up early. Two of the better teams in Lake Oswego, Staff Jennings and GTM Construction, are squaring off for first place in the American League, the majors for 10-, 11- and 12-year-olds.

My son plays for Staff Jennings, and I am one of the three coaches—and six dads—who are part of the team's entourage. Come rain, come shine, come the 10:10PM dousing of the Westlake lights, the six of us are always there, lugging the equipment bag, reliving the winning rallies, pitching whiffs.

We are there, I think, because we are afraid the day will come when our sons won't be. When the game grows stale, or the kids grow up, and baseball makes us feel old instead of young.

And though we are there for all the boys on the team, our sons are our magnetic north. When the ball veers the sons' way, our eyes narrow, our breathing stops, our prayers begin.

Staff and GTM are both 8–3, earnest rivals but hardly bitter enemies. The kids and coaches are part of the same twilight culture, a fraternity of Sunday afternoon make-up games, dashes to the batting cages and snack-bar dinners.

Whatever enmity exists between the coaches doesn't divide the kids. They're all in awe of Tyler Mildren's three home runs Saturday. They're all helpless when Shane Richins brings the curve. They all whisper the name of Shane's older brother, "Gehrig," as if he were the original Iron Horse.

And the boys are all unfinished, unlimited, unstrung. Fred Schreyer, Staff Jennings' manager, is forever after our kids to cut down on the mental errors, but the truth is that 10- and 11-year-olds are mental errors in cleats.

They can't lay off the high heat. They freeze up when they hear dad screaming from the dugout. They sometimes wake up at 10:10AM for a 9 o'clock game.

About 10:10AM on this particular Saturday, GTM had a 3–0 lead, and Staff Jennings had a runner on first with two out in the top of the sixth.

When Michael Breuer hit a hard grounder to first, the runner, Zach Francis, jumped over the ball to avoid getting hit, then raced on. When GTM's right fielder bobbled the ball, we had runners on second and third with the tying run coming to the plate.

The tying run never got there. With a mighty flourish, the ump, a teeming kettle of fish, called Francis out for interfering with the first baseman's chance to make a play.

It was, all the coaches agreed, a lousy way to end the game, although GTM's crew was much better at masking the disappointment.

They went home with their sons, and we went home with ours, all of us hauling the humbling reminder that as we move on, someone else is calling the balls and strikes.

When your son is victorious, you can lift him up; when he is defeated, you can dust him off. But you have less and less to say about the way your child and the game are going to turn out.

You can only wait helplessly in your cage as he takes the field, floating on the buoyancy of his dreams and anchored by the weight of yours.

THE SHADE OF A FAMILY TREE

THE INVASION OF THE HINNENTHALS, Weispfennings and Brueggemanns—not to mention a boatload of Duins—began late last week and by Saturday, Puget Sound was under siege and Poulsbo, Wash., had fallen.

The clan celebrated that afternoon by gathering in a simple church above Poulsbo harbor and sacrificing one of their young warriors in an ancient cleaving ritual.

The last time I gathered with family in a church and sang "On Eagle's Wings," the family was LaDonna Ann Brugato's, come to Newberg to kiss their daughter goodbye.

That morning, and the aftermath of the Heaven's Gate cult, came rushing back Saturday the moment the soloist cut loose with the hymn.

But this was a happier time: a wedding ceremony and a family of hardy Minnesota stock—my father's—banding together for another summer rally.

Your family may be warming up this weekend for a similar rally, a break in the game of solitaire, a change of pace. We spend too much of our lives with the speed control stuck on "Pause" or "Fast Forward." Last weekend was my time to enjoy the feel of play; I hope this weekend is yours.

You wouldn't know Carmen and Marty, the bride and groom. I didn't either. But I recognized several generations on the right side of the aisle. We all got our start in the same humble place, the beer-and-bratwurst burg of New Ulm, Minn.

My father was the youngest of four siblings who grew up in New Ulm. The three boys all ventured into the service, eventually pitching camp or dropping anchor on one coast or the other.

But the lone daughter, Alice, stayed behind, eventually marrying Mark Hinnenthal, a hardware merchant, and raising his five kids in the nearby town of St. Peter.

Those kids were my cousins, Faith, Kathy, Kristi, Bob and Anne. On the occasional summer when my father hauled us back to the heartland, Faith, Kathy and Kristi were my older sisters, my lifeguards, my homecoming queens.

I still remember the lake. I couldn't have been more than 7 or 8 on the afternoon we sought release from the thick Minnesota heat, but I can still feel the mud in my toes, the water at my chin and my arms around their necks.

When they tossed me in the air, I came down with something I've never lost: the certainty that this family would never let me sink beneath the waves.

My mother's family was Philadelphia at Christmas, my father's Minnesota for the Fourth of July. The Hinnenthals were robust and balanced and adaptable, even if that meant adapting to Alice getting pregnant with Anne at the age of 44. There was always room at their dinner table and never a good reason to hurry off after dessert.

Save for Uncle Mark, who died five years ago, the Hinnenthals were all in Poulsbo last week for the marriage of Kathy's son, Marty. So were my father and his brothers; so were me and the kids.

Some of these relatives my children had never seen before, and some they will never see again, so I was careful with the introductions. I didn't trace the family scars, buried under all those layers of southern Minnesota stoicism. I didn't speak the names of the dead.

It wasn't, after all, the time to go too far back or too far forward. It was a weekend to rest in the shade of the family tree, comforted at the depth of the roots and the breadth of the hammock.

A weekend of joining together to play. When the soloist stood to sing about the refuge and the rock, I sang for the families who need to be reunited and need to be raised. I felt my daughter's head resting on my shoulder. I remembered the lake.

SEPTEMBER 30, 1997

FATHERS AND SONS

MY 12-YEAR-OLD SON IS VISIBLY PAINED by the foolish opinions I hold on the things he loves.

Whenever we debate R-rated movies, video games, the need to inform his sisters that "Hanson sucks," or his inalienable right to roam unleashed at high school football games, his patience with how wrong I am veers toward contempt.

But when the subject is basketball, he still cuts me some slack. He figures I may have something to teach him. Or he knows when he has the ball, we are almost equals, and it only takes a jump shot at the top of the driveway to shut me up.

We've been on the driveway a lot of late. He'll be dribbling by the back of the minivan, asking if I want to play. The most tempting answer to the kids' demands—that knee-jerk "No!"—dies in my throat. I find my sneakers. Give him first outs. Pretend I don't know he'll be going to his right.

We play to 11; you gotta win by two. One night last week Michael drove past me often enough to take a 10-6 lead. "Just think," I told him as I took the ball out, "you win unless I score six straight."

The kid wouldn't look at me, as if afraid that if our eyes met, he'd start laughing, he'd stop wanting to beat me so badly, he'd forget the natural order of things.

I was describing the scene to my father on Friday morning, his 73rd birthday. He and my mom had come down from Seattle for the weekend, and we were heading to Eastmoreland to play golf.

"Do you remember when we played one-on-one?" he asked.

Of course, I said. But the truth is I don't remember all that much. I can see the wooden backboard over our heads and the hook shots he used to toss up with either hand, but I don't remember beating the old man for the first time.

It's been 30 years. It's been a long time since my father tossed me a ball and challenged me to prove something to him.

We survived those days, maybe better than most. When we golf together now, even through the rain that brings the muskrats out onto the banks of Crystal Springs Lake, I think we want the same thing: A shot so unpredictably pure that the impact of the club face and the ball leaves a sweet nothing in the palms of your hands.

We've reached the point, or the sport, where we know it doesn't much matter which one of us swings the club for us both to cherish the moment.

My first glimmer of that bond? When I graduated from the driveway to high school, I didn't have many games that impressed the official scorer, but I can still see my father's face when I popped out of the locker room on a night when everything went right.

He was impressed. And his face was lit by one of those canary-eating grins that said he'd tried not to hope for quite this much, this briefest of moments in which I rose above a game we both loved and he was there to see it.

Near as I can tell, that's the same gratitude I feel now when my father floats a wedge into the shadow of the flag or when my son surprises me with the left-hand dribble.

That game to 11 at the top of the driveway? It didn't end there. Michael tightened up, I tied the score, and we played on. There were times when his intensity in going for a rebound or elbowing me in the back had me laughing out loud.

He didn't hear me. He wanted to win so badly that it was no time to tell him that fathers and sons want the same thing:

For the torch to pass. For the young legs to prevail.

They didn't prevail last week. One of those long jumpers that didn't need to go in finally did, giving the old man a 23–21 victory.

My son dropped to his knees in the driveway. His father gave thanks.

DECEMBER 11, 1997

BOYS' NIGHT OUT
WITH HEROIN GIRL

T HE HOUSE LIGHTS HAD JUST POPPED ON, and "Come On, Eileen" had just died down, when my 12-year-old son stopped gloating long enough to glance my way and ask, with genuine concern, "Are you OK?"

As opposed to what? Deaf? Nauseous? Nostalgic? Still undecided, I let him off with a nod. The night was young. The opening act had cleared the Theater of the Clouds, but the NRK Snowball was just getting rolling.

The story of how three seventh-graders and I came to be in the Rose Garden Tuesday night is one I'll save for the ticket donor's funeral.

But there we were along with The Cure, Save Ferris, Ben Harper and—the kids' hometown heroes—Everclear.

In the mental storyline I've drafted of my son's life, the rock concert chapter didn't come this early. I was 17 before I was initiated into the raucous marvel of festival seating, just in time to see the Stones, Led Zepplin and Jethro Tull play Seattle Center in the summer of '72.

But Michael and his buddies got the bug early. They sleep with Foo Fighters and the Smashing Pumpkins. Roll their eyes at parental advisories. Sneak out to the car early and slip the Mighty Mighty Bosstones into the tape deck so it explodes when Dad hits the ignition.

NRK—94.7 on the FM dial—is their gospel station, so hitting the Snowball was their idea of seventh heaven. Nor were they given pause on the way in when we were stopped and frisked by meat-handed security guards looking for drugs, alcohol or weapons.

I suppose the "meat-handed" really isn't fair. Given the training these guys have had at the NBA player's entrance, the pat-down was rather deft.

The basic color for the evening was black, owing to The Cure. The Rolling Stones of alternative rock, The Cure has been serenading depressed teenagers since the late '70s.

My concert companions weren't in the mood for black. They sang right along when Save Ferris reprised "Come On, Eileen," a song two years older than the boys.

They hooted when the song lyrics piped through the arena between acts were as entertaining as they were objectionable. Michael and Ben displayed the proper amount of shock when Brandon came scrambling back from the men's room to announce, "Hey, there were two guys in there in a stall..."

(Be still my beating heart.)

"...and they were smoking POT!"

And once Everclear took the stage, they didn't even envy the bozos who occasionally would bubble to the surface of the mosh pit.

Watching my son sing along with "Heroin Girl," I was surprised he didn't come out of his chair...the way I used to do when the Boss took a stab at romance and disappeared down Flamingo Lane.

At 10PM, when the roadies were setting up for The Cure, two women in their mid-20s sat down in front of the boys and struck up a conversation. How old are you guys? Where do you go to school? Is your mother picking you up? How do you feel about The Cure?

"We grew up on The Cure," they sighed. "As should you."

Instead, the boys just grew tired. When I glanced over at 11PM, Michael and Ben had their eyes shut. No one argued when I suggested we call it a night. On the way home, Ben said, "You know, if you liked The Cure, I bet you'd be popular in high school."

"If you like The Cure," Brandon countered, "you'd be popular in the retirement home."

As someone who can still name "Thunder Road" or "Thick as a Brick" in three notes, I kept my mouth shut and drove on, occasionally flicking on the high beams for a better view of the road ahead.

DECEMBER 21, 1997

ANOTHER AIRPORT NEAR-MISS

T HURSDAY NIGHT, AND THE WHIRLWIND END of the E concourse. Families are lunging at one another, cameras flashing. The airport reunions are so distracting and so intense that a few moments pass before I realize the girls are gone.

Turning, I scan the crowd, searching for the blue coat or the wild bangs. Before the first heart murmur, I spot Christina 20 feet away, standing by the jumping-off point of the nearest moving sidewalk.

She is waving me over in a "Dad, you gotta see this" sort of way. Her cheeks are flushed, her eyes ablaze. There is no sign that anything is wrong, nor any sign of her younger sister.

Until the crowd shifts, unscrambles, and I see Lauren on the ground. She is sitting with her legs curled under her, just off the spinning edge of the metal sidewalk.

Her gray skirt is caught in its teeth.

I am 15 feet away. I am not moving quickly enough. A businessman with a briefcase bends down and takes Lauren's skirt in his fist. I am at his shoulder when he finds the force to pull it free.

Lauren, still 7, is looking up at me. She cannot imagine what she just missed, but she is sizing up the trouble she sees on my face. And the trouble is bigger than she is.

I spread her skirt out in the palm of my hand. The gray wool is torn apart and scarred with grease. I drop the skirt and lean back against the concourse wall, one lonely thought pushing me toward my knees:

That a moment of neglect almost cost me my little girl?

No, lonelier still: Her mother is going to kill me.

The mother who sent us off, begging me to be careful. To hold the girls' hands in the parking lot. To never let these innocents drift out of my sight.

Like a speeder watching the flashing lights gain on him in the rearview mirror, I suck on a mouthful of lame excuses and discover nothing tastes right.

I pull the girls toward me; they back away from my dismay. For them, the crisis has passed.

They don't see the 7-year-old in Vancouver, Wash., who ran out to greet the recycling truck with a bundle of Christmas cookies in her hands.

They don't remember the 8-year-old girl from Scio who walked out into the rain to get the mail during the flood of '96, and never came back. They don't wonder if disaster, biding its sweet time, is gaining on us with each inexplicable near-miss.

They only want to see their grandmother step off the plane, which already is unloading. The girls crouch behind the agent's desk, hoping to surprise her. Each time Lauren peeks out into the homecoming stream, she laughs out loud.

They watch grown sisters embrace. Mothers reach for their sons, a teenager for her high school sweetheart. A woman in a military school uniform leans into the shelter of her father's arms.

But no grandmother, even when the plane is empty. My mother-in-law must have slipped by us when the man with the briefcase was pulling Lauren back from the edge. She must be lighting flares by now down by baggage claim.

We head back up the E concourse. The first chance they get, the girls are running for the moving sidewalk. They have no fear and no memory.

My bark reins them in. We walk on together, but once again, they don't have my full attention. I am lost with the girl in Vancouver and the child in the rain and the guardians who only glanced away only half as long, and are suffering still.

APRIL 7, 1998

THIS BEING JUNIOR HIGH, TAKE COVER

As WE LEFT THE HOUSE FRIDAY NIGHT, my son's feelings about the upcoming dance and at least two of the chaperones were clear. "Try to stay away from me, will ya?" he asked.

By the time we reached the junior high school parking lot, his instructions were far more explicit:

"Pretend like you don't know me, OK?"

Then he pulled the baseball cap low over his eyes and vanished into the cafeteria, determined to prove he could go it alone into the loneliest days of his life.

Welcome to The Blunder Years. Unless you're cursed with a photographic memory, you tend to forget how awkward, how bizarre, how painfully unforgiving those early teenage years were.

Then the lights go out and the DJ pops up, and you watch a whole new platoon of kids stumble through the nightmare.

This is, after all, junior high, when life doesn't have a beat you can dance to. I haven't forgotten Sadie Hawkins with Holly Wheeler, when we were locked into so many consecutive slow dances that the back of her sea-blue dress stuck like wet tissue to the palm of my hand.

But that was high school, when I wasn't still trapped in clothes that didn't fit and a body that wouldn't follow instructions.

Friday's Swing Dance was sponsored by Lake Oswego Together, a group dedicated to convincing teenagers that drugs and alcohol are an open elevator shaft, not a stairway to heaven.

The lobby doors opened at 7PM. The exits were sealed and locked an hour later, mere minutes before the kids realized the dance, like most other forms of self-expression, was a potential disaster and began probing for a way out.

Unable to find one, they mingled, cavorted or withdrew. The evening had no official uniform. There were sneakers and 3-inch platform wedgies, formal gowns and cutoff jeans, chapped lips and lipstick.

And just beneath the restless surface was a riptide of nervous energy, the turbulence of kids trapped between horseplay and hormones.

For an hour, many took a stab at dancing, flinging themselves at one another like sumo wrestlers or spinning across the floor in two-person teams of crack-the-whip. The girls were by far the most aggressive; when they couldn't find their match among the baseball-capped wallflowers, they partnered with their best friends.

But even when the swing beat surrendered to Whitney Houston and the soundtrack from *Grease,* the kids began retreating to their separate corners, dividing into uneven lots. You had the young man no one would talk to crying by the pop machines. You had the future swimsuit models contemplating their budding power.

And in the strangest of the group dynamics, you had the guys who pass for junior-high cool sprawled on a bench in the lobby and at least two dozen girls arriving to plop down, quite literally, at their feet.

The boys were too self-absorbed to appreciate their audience, the girls too young to be embarrassed by their idolatry. For 10 minutes they held the pose, close enough to touch and too close to speak.

Pretend like you don't know me, OK?

That's easy enough. This being junior high, these kids don't yet know themselves.

They only know—usually in their heads, rarely in the heart—their parents don't have a clue...which means you and the rest of the baffled chaperones must wait in the wings with the other unwelcome guests.

Hang tough. Hang loose. If you never know when those you love will hit bottom, you need to keep one hand free for the rip cord and the parachute.

JUNE 16, 1998

ONE MOMENT, YOU'RE UNDERWATER; the next, you're riding a wave.

Three weeks ago, the May monsoon finally lost steam and baseball returned to this part of the planet. In the wink of a waterlogged eye, my rat pack of 12- and 13-year-olds went from cursing the clouds to kicking the dirt, from playing no baseball to playing nothing but.

The game presents a whole new set of problems when you're forced into action. Not until we started playing four times a week did I realize we had one kid genetically programmed to hang out the car window and yell, "I say a little prayer for you," at pedestrians on the drive to away games.

As I've said before, I'm not a baseball guy. I'm a rookie when it comes to the vagaries of the game, and I can't always prime my players. When my regular catcher went down with a raw knee at the end of May, I devoted an entire practice to prepping his replacement.

Unfortunately, I didn't warn the new catcher to come to Westlake Park prepared. When I told him to set up behind the plate, his face went blank.

"Uh, coach," he began, "I don't have my cup."

Well, I said, let's send someone home to get it.

"But coach," he said, his panic rising, "my cup's in Beaverton."

Where all good cups belong, I thought. Not knowing where else to turn, I called across the diamond to my son, asking to borrow his.

The question set our relationship back several years.

Our fascination with baseball suggests you can't prepare for the sudden turns, the bad hops, the cerebral hiccups. We beat Oregon City by scoring 7 runs in our last at-bat; we lost to Tualatin when they twice scored from third on dropped third strikes.

And the entire coaching staff went brain dead in a third game, failing to protest when West Linn ran off the field at the end of an inning with only two outs.

By the time our scorekeeper woke me up, I'd already brought our runners in. Desperate to shift the blame, I bellied up to the umps.

"Did you know there were two outs?" I asked.

"Yep," the home-plate ump said.

"Aren't you supposed to tell us?"

"Not unless you ask."

You can't dwell on those moments, lest you succumb to what an old football coach once called "paralysis by analysis."

Instead, you focus on guys such as Brendan.

Brendan was what you call your lower-round draft pick. I'd never seen him play. Didn't know his parents. Didn't expect much. I certainly didn't expect a savagely bright shortwave radio enthusiast who's up nights talking to the world.

"How ya doing today?" I'll ask Brendan when he hops off his bike.

"Fine," he says, "considering it's the ninth anniversary of Tienemen Square."

Early last week, I gathered the team at the edge of the infield for a pre-game pep talk. "These guys are good," I said. "You gotta jump on 'em early. You get a big lead and I guarantee they'll go, in the words of a Portland mayor, 'Tits up.'"

Everyone laughed save Brendan.

"Vera Katz said that?" he asked.

Maybe if we make that road trip to the state playoffs, I'll introduce these guys to Bud Clark. Last time I checked, Brendan was batting .428 and lecturing our infield on Neville Chamberlain and the perils of appeasement.

Last time I checked, we'd won more than we'd lost. We were swinging the bats, squashing the bugs, enjoying the sun and stopping off, in the twilight after each game, at the Tillamook Ice Creamery for double scoops and waffle cones.

That may not mean a thing to a billion people in China—but Brendan is working on changing that, even as we speak.

ANOTHER DAY AT THE BEACH

FIELD TRIP. FIELD...TRIP. If you can't attend the wedding of those words without hearing John Belushi bellow, Food fight! we grew up in identical school districts.

The one field trip I remember from those years was a pilgrimage to New York City, highlighted by an inexplicable detour through the Bowery. The boys on the bus responded with predictable aplomb, hanging out the windows and berating the drunks on the sidewalk.

Kids say the darnedest things.

Early Thursday morning, 150 third- and fourth-graders at Uplands Elementary in Lake Oswego boarded four Raz troop carriers and embarked on Carol DeBoer's biennial invasion of Cannon Beach.

This was the third such westward advance for one of my kids, and the first time I'd outwrestled my wife for a seat on the bus. If I was expecting a day at the beach, I was assigned five young guerrillas and a clipboard with more investigative chores than your average columnist performs in a month.

We were on the road for almost two hours—and as is so often the case in Oregon, two hours weren't enough time to prepare us for what was waiting at road's end.

Not dark alleys and dead-end kids, but a beach deserted by all save the fog. Jellyfish plastered like cowpies on the sand. Gulls lent a sense of elegance by the wind. A whale beyond the breakers.

Even with a stop at Dairy Queen on tap, the end of the rainbow for the kids was the tidal pools by Haystack Rock. We arrived at low tide, giving us complete, if brief, access to the barnacled haven of sea urchins, tube worms and pink sea anemone.

For a good hour, an especially good hour, the 8- and 9-year-olds stepped in puddles and peeked under rocks. Some were on starfish safari, others in the mood for crab, still others content to poke at the puffed-up anemone, lurking like discarded candy lips at the bottom of the pools.

But the common refrain that bounced off the rocks was, Mrs. DeBoer! Mrs. DeBoer!—a desperate plea for her to drop whatever else she was doing and examine some new discovery before it slipped away.

DeBoer, the head of the schools third- and fourth-grade teaching team, spent the hour scampering over the jagged landscape, pulled this way and that to answer a question, verify a sighting, or veto an adoption attempt.

For the most part, I kept my platoon quiet, at least until we upended a mussel-bound rock and found a 4-inch-long cousin of the millipede trying to bury its pointed head in the sand.

I couldn't help myself:

Mrs. DeBoer, Mrs. DeBoer...

We couldn't take the sea beast with us. That's one of the rules: You can't leave the beach with anything save the sand on your shoes. Everything but the trash was left where we found it, chum for the next high tide.

I doubt anyone left the coast empty-handed. When we came off the beach for lunch, my daughter, Lauren, was a bundle of small cuts. Barnacles had taken small bites out of one hand and both legs, so I left her on the bus with her sack lunch and her buddies and carried my sandwich down to the edge of the dunes.

The gulls had gathered. I was treating the two most patient scavengers to bits of kaiser roll when I felt a hand on my back.

Lauren, pigtails to the wind, swung around my shoulder and sat down beside me. I was worried you might be lonely, she said.

You know what I always say, I told her: I'm happier with you than without you.

Her arms tightened around mine. And we sat there, just the two of us, alone in a crowded classroom at the edge of the deep, deep sea.

AFTER THE SIXTH-GRADE DANCE

WHEN I WALKED INTO THE ELEMENTARY school gym Friday night, the breathless question on everyone's mind was the same: "Why Must I Be a Teenager in Love?" That wasn't hard to figure. Heck, everyone was singing along.

In the hours before the annual winter dance, the kids were wondering, "Where can I borrow a poodle skirt?" or asking, "Will my black shoes mark the gym floor?" They were pondering who might win the big swing contest now that Nicole Hasson has graduated.

You couldn't help but enjoy this last gasp in the age of innocence. After the dance—that is to say, after sixth grade—the questions get a lot tougher, thanks to those teenagers in love, in pain, in a hurry.

For the parent of a 13-year-old, Friday night was a reminder of the sweet life. There was an 8:30 curfew. No one hassled the security at the door. Moms and dads were everywhere: At this stage, it's the odd parent who's out of the swing of things.

The whole affair was a far cry, in other words, from a gathering 24 hours earlier at Lake Oswego Junior High: A speaker's forum hosted by the PTA and featuring Les Youngbar, Oswego's chief of police, and two Portland captains, Mike Garvey and C.W. Jensen.

This one played without a soundtrack. The topics—Measure 11, Miranda readings and the local party houses where the beer is in the garage and the parents are in the dark—suggested how much the stakes change in a year or two.

And the questions from the junior high kids—at least from those who didn't already have all the answers—reminded me how much more intent most teenagers are on demanding rights than accepting responsibility.

Not my son, mind you...or yours. I hope it goes without saying that these and all future observations about teen trauma aren't based on personal experience. The angst I'm feeling is strictly vicarious, the emotional contagion of parents who see their child in the distance and don't remember moving.

Maybe you've been there. He's asking when you're going to take him to see *Payback,* or at least buy him tickets to the R-rated bomb; you're asking when he'll ever get around to filling the recycling bin.

She's asking you to drive out to Milwaukie to pick her up from the midnight laser-tag marathon; you're wondering about the force field that prevents her from moving the dirty dinner plate from the table to the dishwasher.

He's demanding the carte blanche and free rein that befits a lad of his age...even as he's screaming for you to run upstairs and remove the midget spider from his bedroom wall.

You have never been so clueless; they have never been so self-absorbed.

And when you try to bridge the gap with a softball question—something along the lines of "Why are you acting this way?"—the look on their face reminds you that they have absolutely no idea.

This is all new to them, too.

Jensen, the father of a 14-year-old, had some sage advice last week at the junior high:

Parent and teenager need a collaborative mission statement, he said. They need a partnership, with a clear understanding of which party is the CEO with a controlling interest. And if teenagers need to be empowered, they also need to be accountable.

I remember the parents nodding. I remember the teenage prisoners fidgeting, increasingly annoyed that they weren't being entertained.

Which reminds me: If you still have a child with a ponytail and a poodle skirt, enjoy the dance. For as long as it lasts.

PARALYZED BY ALL THEIR PROSPECTS

THE INITIAL FLURRY OF HAND WRINGING, face painting and ear tweaking is meaningless. The gestures are feints, illusions, third-base theater. Nothing matters until the coach flashes the indicator, the batter's signal to pay attention.

The cue may be a brush of the forearm or a thump on the chest. What follow are the marching orders for the batter and the base runners. Bunt down the first baseline. Steal. Hit-and-run.

Standing in the coaching box by third base, filled with self-importance, you go through the motions and shout a little encouragement.

Then you stand and watch while those intrepid 14-year-olds freeze up, blank out or just plain ignore you.

In my first year out on the field flashing signs, I'm still getting used to these communication breakdowns. And 14 games into our season—the last year of organized ball for most of these young men—I finally have realized they are simply too distracted by growing up.

They are semi-paralyzed by all their prospects, the particulars of which we might pick up on if only parents and teenagers could develop a system of hand signals as precise as those that convey the varied options of baseball.

A four-game winning streak finally brought our Lake Oswego junior-baseball team back to break-even last week, but it's been a rough year. In one numbing stretch, we were outscored 41-8 in a trio of losses. Our gloves and bats were greased with ball repellent; our base runners forever leaning the wrong way. Our only defensive stopper was the infield fly rule.

And the horror show seemed to bother the coaches more than it bothered the kids. There were times, I confess, when they were so loose and goofy in their stretching drill that, fungo bat in hand, I circled the squad like Al Capone in *The Untouchables*, sorely tempted to impose some gangster discipline.

We beg them to focus, then belatedly realize they don't focus as they used to because there's so much more to focus on. What's going on in their heads? Baseball suddenly has company: Heather Graham. High school. Hormones in hyper-drive. Who's to say?

"Conor ♥s Lindsay" appeared last week in Carolina blue block letters on our first baseman's arm, but generally these guys don't wear their hearts on their sleeve.

Maybe they're missing signs because they're searching the bleachers for a father and not finding one. Maybe they don't jump at the chance to steal because chicks dig the long ball, and they reached first on an infield single.

As the season has rolled on, I've relaxed my expectations. I've accepted that all these guys won't make it at the high school level, and I've begun to enjoy the moments when their instincts take over, and they make a play you can't coach.

And I'm taking solace in the words of Pat Jordan, who rocketed out of high school as a $50,000 bonus baby back in 1959, then crashed and burned without ever making the show.

"As a young pitcher," Jordan writes in his new book, *A Nice Tuesday*, "I missed every nuance, every small satisfaction, every significant moment that makes life worth living, because I so lusted after the biggest ones. Success, fame, recognition, certitude. I had to prove I was the best....

"But I have learned my lesson over the years. Now, as an old man, I delight in nuances, small moments, delayed gratifications, unrealized expectations. I have taught myself to get my satisfactions from the smallest gifts, the most distant possibilities."

As an aging coach, maybe I've been reminded, too, that these 14-year-olds are still young and full of lust. They are still seeking success, fame, recognition and certitude.

And more times than I care to imagine, they have flashed their old man an indicator. The cue may be a sudden fury or a sullen silence or a question that hangs out there like a timid curve ball—but it's a desperate signal to pay attention that's followed by the angst they can't put into words.

Then they stand there and watch while we freeze up, blank out or just plain ignore them.

OCTOBER 19, 1999

HOMECOMING:
A NIGHT TO REMEMBER

THE CORSAGE, I THINK, was the perfect emblem of the evening.

The white roses took everyone's breath away. When my 14-year-old son first realized the Homecoming bouquet would cost $17.50, he began hyperventilating.

And when Michael stood in front of his date Saturday night, preparing to attach Courtney to the corsage, I had the same shortness of breath.

"Are you sure you don't want to help him put that on?" I asked my wife.

"It's a wrist corsage," Nancy said. "It goes on her wrist."

Oh.

Too many high-school rituals, I'd argue, pin the student body on the sidelines, leaving most of the teenagers feeling like second-stringers on the freshman football team, wondering whether they're ever going to get into the game.

That's why I have to hand it to Michael and several of his friends: They decided to take Homecoming by storm. Buckle up in the eye of the hurricane and ride the weekend for all it was worth.

Given that their festivities involved a party of eight, that required the kind of preparation that normally attends the Group of Seven. Dinner reservations.

Floral arrangements. An elaborate transportation grid designed, Michael assured me, to keep the girls from ever seeing the inside of my van.

Where did the parents fit into this drama? We were the bit players: the finance company, the catering service, the chauffeurs, the paparazzi, the dumbwaiters.

But, hey, this evening wasn't about us. The theme of the evening was breaking away. The guys' attitude was, I can handle this...at least I can if you loan me thirty bucks.

The match game went off, best we could tell, with surprising ease. The guys got their bids in early: Adam and Kendra. Evan and Natalie. Trent and Alexandra. Michael and Courtney. I would never have been able to keep that straight except that Alexandra's parents invited the Homecoming couples and their parents over Saturday evening for a pre-game show, complete with hors d'oeuvres.

The boys didn't eat. The boys were hard-pressed to get up off the couch when the girls finally came downstairs, coifed to kill, and introduced a little elegance into their young lives.

For the next 10 minutes, the moms and dads bounced off one another, jostling for position in the group-photo shoot. My flash was still warm when the kids were out the door, bound for a 7:15PM dinner at Bugatti's Ristorante in West Linn.

We all had places to go, but no one was in a hurry to move. Evan's mother returned from the chauffeuring duty to Bugatti's to report that my son had handled things well when the girls decided they weren't going to order very much.

"Don't do that," Michael said. "Order what you want. I have plenty of money."

Of course he did. He had my thirty bucks.

The final anecdote of the evening? When two of the parents drove back to Bugatti's at 8:45 to transport the troupe to the high school dance, the eight freshmen were just being served dinner.

The parents decided to wait in the parking lot. After five minutes, a waitress came out with two glasses of white Zinfandel.

Kids order the darnedest things.

How did the evening go and the corsage hold up? What of the dance? The farewell scenes at the front door? I don't really know. I don't think I'm supposed to know. Michael was home by midnight, but he didn't come back to talk about his date, only to pick up his sleeping bag, pillow and Nintendo gear for a team sleepover at Trent's.

He couldn't wait to be gone again. A minute or two after the door closed, I walked outside to find him sitting in the dark of the front yard, waiting for his ride.

"Why don't you at least stand under the streetlight?" I asked.

"I'm fine here," Michael said.

And he probably was. After all, the night was still young and the old man didn't have the legs to follow him all the places he planned to go.

JANUARY 1, 2000

REVENGE OF THE READING CONTEST

Revenge is sweet.

Reading is bliss—"I have always imagined that Paradise will be a kind of library," Jorge Luis Borges once said—but revenge is sweet.

Three years after I went up in flames in the family's first reading contest, I challenged my children to a rematch.

Lest you've forgotten the first book brawl, I bet my kids—at a nickel a page—that I could read them under the table in the 15 weeks before Christmas. Little did I imagine that Michael would be Machiavellian enough to sneak off with R.L. Stine.

Stine writes adolescent horror fiction, most notably the *Goosebumps* books. He's Dean Koontz without the big words. By reading forty-odd Stine books, Michael cleaned my clock. He got rich. I plotted my comeback.

Still driven by the anachronistic notion that there is something more enduring in the written word than what's available on Nintendo 64 or the *World Wrestling Federation Raw*, I proposed a second contest last January.

All comers. A year-long affair...with one small caveat to offset the R.L. Stine factor.

Certain books, I announced, would earn double pages for the kids. Books of unquestionable quality. The books I love. Classics.

Like *The Hobbit?* Christina asked. Of course.

Or *Lonesome Dove?* Lauren groaned. You better believe it.

"How about *Buried Lies* by Peter Jacobsen?" Michael asked.

I'm sorry, kid, but we have to draw the line somewhere.

They left the starting blocks in a rush, the girls in the company of *Ella Enchanted* and *Chelsea and the Green-Haired Kid*, Michael on sniper patrols with Stephen Hunter.

They read Walter Farley and Laura Ingalls Wilder, Jack London and Harper Lee, Stephen Ambrose and Olive Ann Burns. Michael tagged along with John Feinstein on *A Good Walk Spoiled*, Lauren solved the *Dollhouse Murders*, and Christina clung to *My Side of the Mountain*.

Dear old Dad had fun with Dutch Leonard in their wake, biding his time, waiting until summer vacation. In one week on the Jersey shore, I polished off 2,000 pages of Dean Koontz—his words aren't that big after all— and Stephen King while the kids wrestled with the waves and saltwater-logged foam footballs.

By the time we returned home, the 1999 reading contest was a race for second place.

At contest's end, Lauren, my fourth-grader, had consumed 8,878 pages, edging her brother by the width of *The Silver Chair*. ("Did you check her math?" Michael wanted to know.)

All told, the kids read 85 books, not a single one by R.L. Stine. Far too few, I suppose, were classics, but even the mediocre books seemed to increase their appetite for the stories worth their weight in chocolate.

We were no longer counting pages, after all, on the after-Christmas train ride to New York City when I found Lauren bent over *Harry Potter*, Christina deep into Jon Krakauer's *Into Thin Air* and Michael all wrapped up in some video-game magazine.

Two out of three ain't bad.

Although it is true that my children have not yet asked for the stepladder so they can climb through our library toward the paradise of the upper shelves, their handprints are on the wall at the downtown Borders. As much as they enjoy playing hide-and-seek at Powell's, they also know the best places to turn a few pages while they're waiting to be found.

And each time I crept upstairs last year to kiss them goodnight and found them peeking at me over a book jacket, happy to see me but pained by the interruption, giggling that they were gaining on me, I had my revenge against a world that thinks the written word is fading, a future resigned to the notion that we'll spend the next millennium drawing all our inspiration from a television or computer screen.

Reading is bliss. And sweet revenge.

MARCH 5, 2000

I CAN'T BLAME THE BLAZERS. Can't lay it off on John Rocker or the latest hockey slashing. No NFL felon or salary dispute can explain why I took five separate trips to the Chiles Center last week to watch the 4A girls' state basketball tournament.

Maybe it's a father-daughter thing, this preference for what girls bring to sport. I have two daughters who dream of following Brandy Mortenson or Sharon Van Eaton into that building.

And the father—or, at least, the sentimentalist—in me goes out to the overachievers from West Albany and the bumper-car basketball of Milwaukie.

To Lake Oswego freshman Anna Martin, when she's asked to guard all-state senior Betsy Boardman.

To Oregon City's Buffy Hummel, who can't hear the pressure gaining on her.

And to Springfield's Chelsea Wagner, who stepped onto the court against Westview in the first round and missed all 13 of her shots in an overtime loss.

As I write this, late on Friday night, the state championship game between Westview and Crater is still 20 hours away. Two dozen girls are staring at the ceiling, wondering how to stop the Cats' Kara Braxton or the Comets' raucous sophomores.

But I've already seen enough to have gained a reprieve from everything that is tired and stale in sport and everyone who is just going through the motions.

I got to watch Anna Martin battle Boardman to the very end of their quarterfinal tournament game, the final minute of which saw the 5-foot-9 freshman make a crucial steal, then get whistled for double dribbling; calmly sink two free throws that gave the Lakers the lead; commit the foul that put Boardman on the line for the game's winning shots...

Then hug her father, Jim, in the lonely hall outside the Laker locker room.

"When I played, I was a psychopath," Jim Martin said. "With her, I can never tell whether they're winning or losing by the expression on her face. But this one really hurt her."

I had the privilege of seeing Hummel, the Pioneers' deaf, determined senior wing, step up—just as she did a year ago—to take the last-second shot that would have tied or won the game.

And I was parked on the sidelines when Wagner, Springfield's leading scorer, returned to the scene of her shooting nightmare. Had even one of her 13 shots fallen in that game against Westview, nothing in this tournament would have been the same.

She never quit, of course. She dug in on defense and chased down rebounds. "I didn't want to lower my head," Wagner said. "For an hour after the game, I was really wound up, thinking about it and what I could have done differently.

"Then I was over it. I moved on."

She moved through dinner with her teammates at the Mongolian Grill, then back to the Holiday Inn Express to finish her math and Spanish homework.

And when she returned to the Chiles Center on Thursday and Friday, Wagner hit 14 of her 29 shots and scored 37 points in two consolation victories.

I would never argue that girls' high-school basketball in Oregon is without flaws. There are too many transfers and too few women coaches. There are too few jumpshots and too many flops to the floor by all-state candidates.

But there is just the right amount of attitude and purpose and optimism.

"You have to remember they're 15-, 16-, 17-year-old kids," said Springfield coach Charlie Olds. "When you want them to be serious about a game, they have a tendency to enjoy the atmosphere. It frustrates me at times that they are pretty loose going into a game...But they help me keep the game in perspective."

They help a lot of us maintain our balance.

After 25 years of watching games, I still get pumped when the Lakers are in town or the Tar Heels are at Duke or when Tiger Woods is on the first tee at Augusta.

But my heart goes out for the girls who volunteer to guard the star or take the last shot; who charge off the Crater bench looking like refugees from the movie *Hoosiers,* then play like Larry Bird; and all the daughters who take their sport so personally that they give basketball the personality fans and fathers can't live without.

LOOKING OUT AT
ALL THAT'S DISAPPEARED

On AN OTHERWISE TRANQUIL SATURDAY afternoon, I took the splitting maul to the swing set.

The ax wasn't my first choice. I opened with a socket wrench, only to find the bolts rusted into the locked and upright position. Next came the crowbar and a hacksaw, but the screw tops kept diving into the grass where only the mower might find them.

So, I went for the maul in that final hour, swinging from my heels to bring the swing set to its knees.

My daughters, Christina and Lauren, now 12 and 10, were nervous spectators, trapped between their allegiance to this docile, stoic part of our backyard and the temptation to don hard hats and join the demolition crew.

They couldn't resist the temptation. After I used the ax blade to cut the wooden rungs on the climbing structure, they took turns knocking the rungs loose with a hammer. Her father's child with tools, Lauren swung it like a softball bat. "Stop choking up," I kept reminding her.

I chose an afternoon when my wife, Nancy, was gone to take the swing set out. It arrived, after all, when Michael, now two weeks shy of snaring his learner's permit, was in kindergarten. A friend named Chris Shepanek helped me piece the wooden giant together.

In the beginning, the Kids' Creation set had the 7-foot-high climbing structure, a rope ladder, a slide, 10 feet of monkey bars and the usual variety of swings.

Not everything held up equally well to the damage children do. Christina took the "horsie" for its last ride several summers back. The girl who sat on the bar above the rings and broke it, years ago, is the president of next year's sophomore class at Lake Oswego High School.

But even after it lost some of its original parts, the swing set was that rare adventure with enough options and flexibility to entertain several kids at once. It was big enough to persuade mine they had better things to do than belittle one another. Now and then (as strange as this may sound), it gave them reason to laugh together.

When I dragged out the Mickey Mouse sprinkler, the slide became the entry chute for a salacious slip 'n' slide. The monkey bars were Christina's chance to beat her older brother to a place beyond their reach. Whenever Lauren wanted to talk to the boys next door, she climbed up into the crow's nest to peer over the fence.

In more recent summers, however, the swing set and the kids began to show their age. There was still the occasional game of "Mountain Climber" or "Hot Lava," but the set had a harder time keeping its balance when teenagers jumped on its bones. It slowly became a bother, an obstacle in the wiffleball games, a nemesis for the mower.

The spiders nesting in the yawning cracks in the wood were seldom disturbed.

It was time to move on, I told myself, as I went searching for the tools. When the maul finally brought one end of the monkey bars down, the girls scampered up the ladder as if it were the north face of the Eiger. Then, we finished dismembering the old bird and threw the broken wings into the back of the van.

The set didn't go gently, but it did go quietly. Even as it was torn apart, I never heard the scream that so marked its tenure: "Daddy! Look!"

Lauren drove with me to the Metro transfer station in Oregon City and helped me bury the frayed remains of the swing set in that unmarked grave. I came back expecting to find all sorts of new room and possibilities, but, strangely enough, the backyard looked smaller, as if it were missing the essential piece that supplied its character.

Nancy was quiet when she got home. There was a moment Sunday when we stood together at the kitchen sink, looking out at all that's disappeared.

She leaned against me, but only for the briefest moment.

When the afternoon sun drops behind the holly trees, I still hear the swing set sing and see the shadow of its passing in the grass. What I miss are the days when my children would leap for the bars or the stars with utter abandon, and I knew where they would land.

JANUARY 4, 2001

CLUELESS IN SUBURBIA
AND CLOSER TO HOME

IF THERE WAS ANY DOUBT—and there wasn't—that beer and wine have been seeping into the neighborhood and my 15-year-old's ragged circle of friends, the matter was settled by the group's first minor-in-possession arrest in late December.

Before the next one—in your backyard or mine—a quick story to bring us all up to speed: Two good friends sent their daughter off to college several years ago, convinced they'd carefully monitored her access to alcohol. She had a curfew throughout high school, and when she did get home from her nightly rounds, her father was always waiting up, a loving but watchful eye on her entrance.

Not long ago, their daughter confided she was much the teetotaler in college; she'd done all her serious drinking in high school. They were stunned. How was that possible, her mother asked: We were so careful . . .

"Oh, Mom," the young woman said, "you and Dad were clueless."

Let's stop kidding ourselves: Most parents are clueless, some (pathetically) by design. And our teenagers are determined to keep us that way. They have figured out that knowledge is power and assume our power over them is limited by our knowledge of their movements.

What we don't know, in other words, can't hurt them.

The kids haven't figured out that in the absence of information, parents are more motivated by perception (what we fear) than reality (what they're doing).

What one neighborhood sophomore was doing on the night of the Christmas dance was slurping a little beer and wine in the back of a car. He was at a party. He and a couple friends wandered off. On their way home, 'round about 1:00AM, a cop pulled their car over and asked if they'd been drinking.

Being good kids, they said, "Yep."

Mom got the rude wake-up call. "I feel so naive," she told me. "I trusted him. I feel it's kind of my fault. I didn't think any of this was possible so soon. Not at 15. I gave him more responsibility and freedom than a 15-year-old can handle. He took full advantage of it."

All together now: Duh.

The young lad is now grounded. So is his mother, grounded in the staggering occurrence of alcohol use. The 2000 Oregon Public School Drug Use Survey reports that 26 percent of eighth-graders and 42 percent of 11th-graders had chugged a cold one in the last 30 days.

That works out, clueless parents, to more than one on your block, if not in your upstairs bedroom.

As you're probably asleep at the switch, let's review the basics:

Most of our teens, even the brightest overachievers, are in a self-obsessed fog, one as unnerving as any that director John Carpenter unleashed upon Jamie Lee Curtis and Antonio Bay.

They've been lectured *ad nauseam* about drugs and alcohol, but more powerful forces are coming into play in their lives. Sex is a startlingly significant factor in drinking; most teenage sexual activity happens when drugs or alcohol have been consumed.

Vigilant parents need to intervene. But even the most vigilant need to recognize that their teenagers are often caught up in a random, haphazard social scene. Because it's hard to find transportation, they often end up in the wrong car. If they're headed for a chaperoned party, it only takes a single cell-phone call to send them winging across town to a house where the kegs outnumber the hall monitors.

What's worse, many parents make for lousy chaperones. Some think teenage drinking is an inevitable rite of passage. Others are so desperate to look cool in the children's eyes, or to promote their teen's popularity, that they're sanctioning coed sleepovers.

What can you do? Snap out of your trance. Stop pretending your child is too good a kid to make a stupid mistake.

Talk to your teenager . . . or find the parents who can talk to theirs. Network. Don't believe anything unless you have two sources. Even if you're convinced you can trust your child, don't trust the crowd he runs with.

Be afraid. Very afraid. You may not live longer, but your teenager will.

FEBRUARY 6, 2001

THE ROAD LESS TRAVELED
DUCKS THROUGH SEASIDE

As WE SLOWLY RETREAT FROM playing the game—often out of respect for it—spectator sport offers two options. We can gravitate toward the showcase of perfection or, in far lonelier gyms, the struggle with imperfection.

One road offers the occasional glimpse of Michael Jordan, Tiger Woods or a clever Super Bowl commercial, but it also drifts, painfully, past Rasheed Wallace, Mark Chmura, the XFL and the celebrated Ray Lewis. The other road meets the ocean at Seaside.

On winter weekends, Seaside is not a destination but a last resort, a hodge-podge of empty trinket shops, wet sand and dull outlet stores. The natives are friendly and the coffee at the Morning Star Cafe has a sweet bite, but they aren't the reason several hundred families head for the beach each Friday night.

No, they come for the youth basketball tournaments.

Kerri and Frank Januik have been running tournaments on the coast since 1993. More than 450 grade- and middle-school teams are playing in the seven on tap this season.

The winter roundball carnivals are a boon for the local economy—Debra Hudson, the manager at the Hi-Tide Motel, estimates she rents between a quarter and half of her weekend rooms to basketball families—and utter chaos for the besieged late-night crew at the Dairy Queen.

Do they showcase great basketball? Of course not. Even at the eighth-grade level, the girls' games are fairly raw, more likely to generate a rugby scrum than an authentic give-and-go. While hard fouls are the rule, "jump ball" is every referee's favorite call.

But in the Seaside gyms, there is a bond between players and spectators that the Trail Blazers would die for. The game is still savagely fresh, not routine and stale. And each encounter with a half-court trap provides relatively painless lessons in how to respond to the intense pressure that waits for these kids down the road.

My bias is showing. What else is new? My eighth-grade daughter and I spent last weekend in Seaside, and I'm returning with my fifth-grader for a second tournament in another 10 days.

But the longer my daughters play, the harder it is to differentiate between them and the other imperfect athletes they meet at midcourt.

I watched all or part of eight games over the weekend, and I was struck by just how fortunate the girls are—to be part of a team, an organism that works best when they work together—and just how fragile.

Maybe the last owes to Seaside's endless running clock, a clock that only stops in the last two minutes of each half for free throws and out-of-bound plays in order to ensure that a new game starts every hour on the hour.

Whenever the girls glance up, the clock is ticking down, and the time they have to savor being 13 and convinced that perfection is still within their reach is disappearing at heartbreaking speed.

That's why long after the scores cease to matter, I'll remember the rainy Sunday morning when six girls gathered in our room at the Hi-Tide to eat maple bars and braid one another's hair while watching a movie together.

And why the most valuable play of the tournament arrived in a 35-point loss, courtesy of an eighth-grader from Seaside named Katie Emmerling.

Late in the first half, Katie and a Lake Oswego player bounced off one another going for a loose ball by the scorer's table. When the ball careened into the stands, the referee was quick to admit she had no idea who'd touched it last.

Without the least hesitation, Katie piped up, "It was off me."

The referee blinked, then waved her away. It doesn't work that way, she said. There are rules, a procedure. We have to abide by the possession arrow.

All of which is true. As any number of smug, professional, semiperfect lugs prove on a regular basis, you can't always count on an athlete to do the right thing. The games don't always honor honesty and grace.

Ah, but the things that do—as Katie Emmerling already knows—are the things that matter.

IN THE ABSENCE OF WORDS,
STATS BIND THE WOUNDs

I WAS FURIOUS WITH MY SON WHEN I left the house Tuesday night and fuming when I returned, muttering, discouraged by his self-absorption and his frightening resemblance to who I probably was in the summer of my 16th year.

I didn't want to talk to him. I didn't want to hear his latest demand on my time or my Durango. But no sooner had I collapsed at my desk than he came through the door, got right in my face and said:

"Did you see Rivera blew the save?"

I grunted in feigned nonchalance, even as I reached for the channel changer and flicked on *Baseball Tonight*. The kid nodded, knowing he had my full attention: "And Boone already has two home runs."

Two more dingers? The conversation was on. We were back with our mental calculators and lineup cards in the world of fantasy baseball.

Our safety zone.

Our bridge over troubled waters.

Someone reminded me not long ago that if you replayed everything you said to your teenagers, you'd be amazed at how much of it is negative.

That stands to reason. Your tone is perfectly in keeping with their attitude.

There's been, of late, a sudden surge in the bleating that we're terrified of our teenagers.

Baloney. My experience has been up-close and personal, and I'm not afraid of this crew—I'm discouraged. Stunned by the loss of empathy, the ability to appreciate someone else's point of view. Dismayed that my son, a week shy of his 16th birthday, disdains so much responsibility even as he evolves into a 24-hour request line.

OK, so maybe 23. Thank the dear left-fielders for that hour we have with fantasy baseball.

If you're not up to speed on the game, most fantasy leagues allow you to draft a roster of major-leaguers and score points based on their on-field performance. Those leagues were largely water-cooler fodder until the Internet came along and offered to keep the stats.

Michael and I are hooked up to Small World, which counts more than 200,000 active participants in its baseball game. Our division sports 14 high school sophomores, three of whom are proving to be much better bench managers and salary-cap manipulators than the league's lone grizzled veteran.

Are we talking mindless entertainment? Of course we are. But it gives the two of us a reason to care when Kansas City plays Tampa Bay, cause to curse the commercials that interrupt the scrolling game summaries on ESPN's *Bottom Line*...and a mutual interest when we're at one another's throat.

Fifteen is a curious age, and while I've wandered through the curiosity shop before, I've never seen it from this angle. This past year has turned my oldest child into someone I barely recognize, a kid adept at leaving the impression that he couldn't care less about our convictions and our priorities.

The goal is not to take it personally, to grasp whatever time and fragile links remain. Fantasy baseball gives us a little more breathing room. On curfews, study hours, sibling rivalries or the weekend chores, we are forever at odds.

But rookie Albert Pujols? The resurgence of Omar Dahl? The Todd Helton-Jim Thome dilemma at first base? Over these we can quarrel without losing patience or perspective.

In a perfect world, I suppose, I'd be treating my son to peanuts or Crackerjack somewhere along the first-baseline of a ballpark that rivals Camden Yards and Coors Field.

But while major-league baseball remains a pipe dream in Portland that far too few are smoking, my son and I are already going our separate ways, for reasons hardly unique to the two of us. Even as we drift, fantasy baseball keeps us anchored near the same dock, a place where our differences tend to disappear, or cease to matter, in the rush to see if Barry Bonds dumped another one in McCovey Cove.

If you have something else to nurse the stitches in your heart, consider yourself fortunate. If you don't, take my advice and trade for Helton whenever the Rockies play at Coors.

PEACE ON EARTH
AND A GOOD YELL
FOR GOOD MEASURE

AT OUR SEASON-ENDING SOCCER PARTY—now, there's an Oregon oxymoron—the coaches received several lovely parting gifts. I came away with compact binoculars, new cleats and several Starbucks credit cards, a bounty that spoke to the bare essentials of these desperate times: foresight, sure footing and venti lattes.

But the sweetest send-off of the afternoon was a comeback line. Cameron Luck, the head coach of our sixth-grade rec team, was explaining to the parents that I'd served as the "bad cop" during practices, offering a little focus and discipline to the after-school riots.

No one was more annoyed by those daily offerings than my daughter, Lauren, who promptly interrupted Cam to repeat her objection: "I told you, Dad, you yell too much."

"Yeah," piped up Claire Egli, the smallest and most fearless player on the team, "but it's a good yell."

You might think it's a bad sign when an 11-year-old so easily grasps—in a half-dozen words—the awkward weave of your style and your intentions.

But when, in addition, she so eloquently speaks to the dilemma of the season, you duck your head and hand her the lead.

We are confronted by all the usual contradictions of Thanksgiving: The notion that good and plenty are inseparable. The curious habit of celebrating all that we have by eating like a sumo wrestler. That prolonged swing through the buffet line even as we are buffeted by the uncompromising demands of time, family and expectations.

But we are also hobbled by the unique challenges of a nation under attack. On what is traditionally the most heavily traveled weekend of the year, many of us are afraid to fly.

As we gather with our families, it is almost impossible not to reflect on the 3,900 families that were eviscerated in New York, and the countless others that have someone guarding the waves or exploring the caves around the Persian Gulf.

And after arguing, as most of us have for the past 11 weeks, that pacifism is the refuge of the gutless and the misguided, we come now in whispers to the prince of peace.

At a time when there's a lot of useless noise and not much useful direction, I don't think only columnists and coaches are asking: What's the right admonition for these times? What's the appropriate holiday blessing?

What's the telling blend of encouragement and caution? Patriotism and liberty? Revenge and remembrance?

When the United States is hard at war, what qualifies as the "good yell" from the tables far from the front, tables overflowing with the evidence that we're generally on the receiving—not the giving—end?

And how do we find a voice that resonates with more conviction than—like those incessant Salvation Army bells in the crowded doorways of department stores—the annoying twang of a troubled conscience?

I'm guessing the search for that voice won't begin at the edge of the Thanksgiving table. I'm guessing more of the right words will be found while you are scrambling after a football in the early-morning mud than while you are watching the Lions or the Cowboys from the belly of your couch.

While you are inviting the usual turkeys in off the sidewalk than when you are stuffing another Butterball at the kitchen counter.

While you are looking to escape the lonely cocoon of your own thoughts for the company of saints and the sanctuary of friends.

And while you are listening to those who have passed this way before without binoculars and cleats.

I hope you share your prayers Thursday. I hope you speak your mind. I hope you confess your anguish and fill the room with your reckless longing.

And through all that, I hope you have friends and defenders like Claire Egli willing to speak up for you, giving you credit for good intentions, giving you the benefit of the doubt, if only because they've heard, somehow, in the dark coal of your voice, the rough beginnings of diamonds and stars.

DECEMBER 25, 2001

ALLOWING FOR THE
BEST OF INTENTIONS

My 11-YEAR-OLD AND I HAVE a simple understanding that has done wonders for our relationship.

Nothing is her fault. Whenever anything goes wrong, I'm to blame.

When she doesn't finish her homework, it's because I wasn't available. When she makes a mistake on the basketball court, I was putting too much pressure on her. When she doesn't put something away, I failed to give her proper notice.

Lauren, we both agree, is just about perfect. I'm the problem when things don't work out.

You may think me a fool for eliminating the argument over who's responsible for whatever mess we stumble into.

But you'd be surprised at how quickly Lauren becomes unnerved by seeing the burden of blame—and responsibility—placed squarely upon someone she loves. Given a little time and a little room, she invariably, and rather quietly, comes around to an apology and a concession that while she's obviously not a part of the problem, she might be part of the solution.

I offer this, on this Christmas morning, because it has seemed in recent months, since America has gone to war, that far too few adults seem interested in arranging a similar peace.

I'm not talking about compromise in the caves of Tora Bora; I'm all for finishing what al-Qaida started. I am talking about the war at home, the relentless war of words.

Some of the fiercest fighting in the war against terrorism is still being played out on the Op-Ed pages or in the flash-fire world of e-mail. Most of the misplaced aggression is served up by those freedom fighters, apparently too old to re-enlist, who are hunched over their computers, cursing anyone who doesn't share their view of patriotism as being in league with the terrorists.

I used to think the freedom to disagree was one of the freedoms we were proudest of; what's more, that those disagreements were healthy, the whetstones on which we honed our beliefs, not the rocks for our throwing arm.

That theory is being sorely tested.

"The notion that a radical is one who hates his country is naive and usually idiotic," H.L. Mencken wrote several wars back. "He is, more likely, one who likes his country more than the rest of us, and is thus more disturbed than the rest of us when he sees it debauched. He is not a bad citizen turning to crime; he is a good citizen driven to despair."

Mencken is being typically precise...and unusually forgiving. He is peddling an increasingly rare commodity, the benefit of the doubt. He is allowing that someone with whom we passionately disagree may have the best of intentions, not the worst.

That's a daunting leap of faith. I'm not always willing to make it. So I was reminded when a reader suggested I review a pair of year-old year-end conclusions, the first being that George W. Bush was "inarticulate, insipid (and) painfully incidental," the second that the Blazers' Rasheed Wallace had grown up.

My apologies. My bad. My learning experience on the benefit of doubt.

There is a place for outrage, a place we have all visited repeatedly since Sept. 11. There are reasons to remain angry and reasonable channels for our frustration.

But I think we need to reconsider what is pushing all of us to such extremes in the debate over war and peace and all things in between. Perhaps your intentions need a gut-check. Maybe you're the reason things aren't working out. Conceivably, you might end the argument by not assuming the worst but assuming the blame.

These are daunting lessons. I'm still working them out. Thank goodness Lauren is just 11, with plenty of time to school me.

"Justice is the grammar of things," Frederick Buechner argues. "Mercy is the poetry of things." Make no mistake: Justice is essential for the maintenance of order and discipline, not to mention sentence structure.

But it's the poet, not the grammarian, you hope to see bent over your gravestone, slowly chiseling out the final lines of the sonnet that survives you.

JANUARY 6, 2002

ANOTHER ROUND OF
LOST AND FOUND

Because NO ONE WILL EVER MISTAKE St. Mary's Home for Boys for a decent home for the holidays, the mentors spirit the boys away whenever possible. On Christmas Day, Ken Ackerman—the host of *Good Day Oregon*—took Josh to see the movie *Ali*. And on the last Saturday in December, I grabbed Curtis and Josh and carted them over to Lake Oswego High School for a girls' basketball tournament.

We stopped for eggnog lattes on the way to the gym. The boys seemed curious about where Lake Oswego fit in on the map of the metro area. Josh pulled out a poem he'd written about his mother choosing to spend her life with drugs instead of him. They didn't seem particularly hungry, but at halftime of the first game, I gave Curtis five bucks in case that changed.

Because I was keeping the official scorebook for the Centennial-North Medford game, I was shackled to the scorer's table and focused on the game. Curtis and Josh were sprawled in the bleachers on the other side of the gym.

At least they were until midway through the third quarter.

I figured they'd popped out to the concession stand. When they were still gone 10 minutes later, I figured they were shooting baskets in the cold barn that is the high school's old gym.

Only after I'd described the two boys to the police did it sink in that they weren't coming back.

Only after I cruised Pioneer Courthouse Square and the bus stations and began drafting my apology to St. Mary's did I realize the curiosity about area geography was a cleverly disguised question about bus routes to Portland.

In the history of the Boys Home, I'm told, no mentor has ever lost a kid while on an outing.

I lost two.

As I write, five days later, Curtis and Josh are still on the lam. Also missing is my confidence that either mentors or St. Mary's make much of a difference in the lives of the homeless boys over whom they watch.

There's little doubt that Josh was the inspiration behind the run. Over the years, he's bolted from various group homes, including a flight from St. Mary's last August, on his 15th birthday. He's resourceful and resilient on the street. When he was 9 or 10, Ackerman said, Josh stole a Cub Scout uniform from a secondhand store and went door to door, asking for the donations that eventually paid for his bus fare.

Curtis, I guess, simply saw an opportunity, an open door. It was nothing personal. Although I've been his mentor for 29 months, I doubt he thought much at all about how I'd feel contemplating the foolishness of trusting him.

If they are safe, the boys have, at the very least, sabotaged some positive change in their lives. St. Mary's was negotiating a foster home for Josh. Curtis was set to move to a group home in Ashland. You never know. Maybe those changes unnerved them. Maybe they have felt so abandoned for so long that they've lost all faith in the rescue mission.

"Josh has been through so many social workers who have promised him the world and never come through," said Ackerman, who met Josh three years ago. "I asked him once why he liked St. Mary's. He said, 'They make me go to school, they make me go to counseling...and no one tells me I have to hate my mother.'

"I think I've helped him stay at St. Mary's, to let him know there's someone out there who loves him. But he's been there way too long because there's no one out there to adopt him. He's convinced there's no place for him to go."

The boys almost certainly won't be coming back to St. Mary's. There's a waiting list for beds at the home; St. Mary's won't leave their two open much longer. When that door closes, there's always MacLaren, a much less demanding surrogate mother.

When I go back to St. Mary's, it won't be with any expectations. The only thing I know for certain any more is that the checks we write and the time we give in the name of these boys have a better shot of filling the hole in us than of ever filling the hole in them.

FLYING NORTH BY NORTHWEST
AND GAINING ATTITUDE

F LYING? ON MY SIDE OF THE LAKE, the favored mode of transportation is sailing, which is why the gym at Uplands Elementary School was decked out in a nautical theme Wednesday afternoon. It is a 500-yard journey, on a north-by-northwest course, from the elementary school to the high school, and the middle stretch of the voyage—Lake Oswego Junior High—bears "Sailors" as a mascot.

Thus, there were sailboat name tags for the graduation ceremony and small anchors on the tables and nautical signal flags hanging from the rafters. There were also 85 sixth-graders, desperate to move on, fidgeting too much to accept the sluggish drift of a boat.

I am witness to their flight, and "flying" is the word.

On this muggy Thursday morning, our family will say goodbye to 12 years of elementary school. Since the fall of 1990, one or more of my three kids has had a desk at Uplands and, more often than not, a pencil without an eraser.

There have been a dozen Family Fun Days, a dozen Halloween dances and a dozen back-to-school nights. I've lost track of the third- and fourth-grade plays, the jogathons and dunk tanks and soccer practices, but I will never forget the 12 years that turned me into a life-long fan of public schools.

I am, I suspect, your average parent at this bend in the road. As my daughter Lauren leaves Uplands, I have no bad memories, no lingering bitterness, no inkling that the school let my children down.

The only burden I bear is gratitude. In the span of those years, my children had a total of seven teachers—Joseph Montalbano, Carol DeBoer, Linda Nelson, Joel Stuart, Denise Hall, Mike McCarroll and Carolyn McBee—and each one gave the...

Forgive me. I have stared at that unfinished thought for 30 minutes, and I can't squeeze all their gifts into its dying breath.

From the beginning, Uplands was the right blend of the familiar and the unexpected, the short leash and the outdoor adventure, the proving ground and the sanctuary. I might have asked that it last a little longer, but Lauren will have none of that. She sees her brother and sister, both at the high school, sailing off without her. She wants after them. She's embarrassed the elementary school has only three meager hallways. She can no longer stomach the dull fare on the food cart.

And in the thick heat of the gym, she is unnerved that I'm sounding clumsy and sentimental. When I ask questions about her friends or the pictures in her yearbook, she rolls her eyes and flicks me away. On this afternoon, I am unnecessary. I am in the way.

I try not to take it personally. I have seen this happen before, kids realizing that the world has a lot more to offer than a conversation with Dad. I play with the anchor. I adjust the sail. I bend over my strawberry and my brownie, the afternoon's main course, chewing on the fear that my kids may never be this safe, or their parents this secure, again.

One by one, the sixth-graders are moving across the stage, listening to their teachers describe them as poets and artists and gentle souls and Renaissance men. I follow Chloe and Audi, Kelsey and Lauren O., Marissa and Claire, my daughter's unbroken circle of friends. I know they will fly off together, north by northwest, into the ridge of clouds and change.

Given 12 years, you'd think I'd be ready. Given 12 years, I am certainly humbled. Then one of the teachers, Maria Strycker, closes by turning to the parents and whispering, "It's hard to say goodbye. Please take care of my kids." And I am reminded of all that Uplands Elementary School was for me and mine, the enduring comfort of shared custody.

In the humid stillness of that crowded gym, the nautical flags quiver languidly overhead, propelled by the breeze of the departing flights or the occasional nudge from one of the floor fans.

I wish I spoke their language. For all I know, they spell out hope. For all I know, they're reminding me that we have no choice but to sail on.

AUGUST 24, 2003

FROM OUR FAMILY
TO THE TROJAN FAMILY

W HEN IT'S FINALLY TIME TO LET GO, the kids catch most of
the breaks. They're breaking away; we're breaking apart. They go forward,
we go back. They move on to the 6PM freshman floor meeting, the 7PM
pizza party and the late-night tour of the frat houses.

We go back to the car, back to the hotel, back to Oregon. We go back
to the empty room that our oldest child slept in for the past 15 years.

Michael didn't sleep much, admittedly, in the last 40 hours before his
mother and I drove him to Los Angeles and the start of his freshman year at
USC. He has a tight, almost inseparable group of friends, and he struggled
with the goodbyes. We hardly saw him. There were barbecues, a concert,
one last night with the gang at the Powell's.

There was the moment Monday morning, as I was leaving for work,
when I went up to his room because I'd heard him moving around just
before dawn. Michael was asleep, but spread out neatly on the rug between
his desk and the bed were a dozen hand-written letters on formal stationery.

The goodbyes. Most of the piles were two or three pages deep. I saw my
son in a different light, the quiet fog of a lamp, his heart on his sleeve, a pen

in his hand. On the drive downtown, I called Nancy on the cell phone and tried to describe the legacy on his bedroom floor. She kept asking me if I was still there.

Because Michael didn't want to think beyond the end of summer, his mother did almost everything to ready him for the trip. She ordered the linens and catalogued the 200 pieces of mail from the "Trojan family." She bought the shelves, the lamps, the fan, the rugs, the chair, the mirror, the tool set and the maddening array of knickknacks.

I just watched, wondering how we would squeeze everything into the Durango. When I left for Wake Forest 31 years ago, my father drove me to Sea-Tac and put me and two suitcases on a plane. It doesn't work that way any more. You don't leave things to chance.

We left home at 7:30AM Tuesday and reached the California state line just before noon. Owing, I suppose, to the free-for-all of the state's gubernatorial recall election, they weren't checking for fruits and vegetables at the border, and nothing else slowed us down.

Michael slept. We didn't say much. Losing your oldest child to college exposes any number of frayed nerve endings. You wonder if the great journey of your adult life, the odyssey of parenting, is drawing to a close. You feel his vulnerability and your age. You give up your license to be a voyeur on his life, at the very moment when it's certain to get more interesting.

After laying over in Bakersfield, we reached Southern Cal midmorning Wednesday. Given that 3,000 freshmen were rolling in with us, the dorm invasion was surprisingly orderly. And whenever agida came after us, we'd bump into another of the 14 freshmen from Lake Oswego at USC and regain our balance. The Trulls at a gas station and the Bergerons at the drop-off. The Schneiders in the dorm, the Soissons at the ticket office, and the Rosenblooms and Breuers at the bookstore.

I'll be honest. I don't remember a word we said.

As the afternoon wore on, Nancy kept reminding Michael of the painfully obvious and he kept shaking his head, as if to say, "I already know that. Why are you confusing me with Dad?" We made a run over to Ralph's for soft drinks and detergent; I hung the mirror. But the time finally came when we ran out of things to say and reasons to stay behind.

Over the years, 18 all told, I've written quite a few columns about my children. It's not as easy as it used to be. If the parenting dilemmas have grown more desperate, so has my kids' need for privacy. They never asked to be the message board when this father wanted others to know they weren't alone.

Thus, I'll let Michael go quietly. I'll put the camera down, and leave it at this: As my son walked into his dorm after we said our goodbyes, he didn't look back. And you can understand why. He's racing forward.

EPILOGUE

IN A MOMENT... NOTHING IS EVER THE SAME. One moment you're bending with spring break. Santa Monica and the sunset are holding hands in the rear-view mirror. You have the girls in the back seat as you head across town on the 10 to pick your son up for dinner.

Then the cell phone rings.

One moment you're arguing over whether you really want a hotel room that looks out over the raucous tide of Venice Beach. You're searching for the nearest Cheesecake Factory. You're plotting your approach to Disneyland, that fabled "happiest place on Earth."

Then your wife says, "Oh, my God...," her voice frantic and raw, and the girls grow deathly quiet.

One moment you have no worries. You're double-teaming the Times' Sunday crossword puzzle. You're wrestling with the mundane.

Then your wife's left hand grips your wrist, and nothing is ever the same.

The first time Nancy took me home to meet her parents, some 25 years ago, we pulled into their Maryland driveway and I thought I saw Mario Andretti bearing down on us.

"Is that short guy your father?" I asked.

He most certainly was. And he died last week at the age of 67, betrayed by a fragile blood vessel in his brain.

Tony Natelli had almost nothing in common with the guy who married the oldest of his five children.

He could build anything and fix everything. He had a passion for details. He had a voice like Sinatra's. He was a conservative, Catholic developer who worried endlessly about the people who might slip between the things he would build and the things he could fix.

And he was a man of few words. He embodied the counsel of St. Francis, who said, "Preach Christ. If necessary, use words." With Dad, they were rarely necessary.

He was the heart and soul of a complex, ever-expanding family. While I had a simple role in the tumultuous gatherings—comic relief—Dad was the family conscience, the espresso maker, the problem solver, the organizer, the sand-castle construction boss, the leader by example. His marriage to Trudy never wavered over 47 years. The marriages of his five kids now total almost 75 summers. This is no coincidence.

He was so generous to me. When I disappeared with his daughter for the West Coast in 1980, he sent us off in his red Alfa Romeo Spyder. When he realized that I'd bought our first house without ever having the place inspected, he never said a word, instead lending himself to its obvious failings.

Mom and Dad took us to Italy for 17 days back in 1996. That's the only time I remember ever making him mad. We were in Florence. I tried to pick up a check.

That wasn't the way you squared yourself with my father-in-law. You didn't have his resources or his sense of responsibility. You didn't have his instincts or his touch.

What answer could you possibly have for his generosity? Over time, I think I figured it out. You repaid the man by taking care of the people he loved. You answered the call when Tony Natelli wasn't in the room.

One moment he filled the room. He was tending to details. He was living in utter and selfless dignity.

Then the cell phone rings. You are listening to your daughters cry in the car. You are fighting back tears of your own as your son hugs his mother in the lobby of the Radisson Hotel. You are losing that fight each time you remember the words of Anne Lamott, words Dad would have loved for their heartfelt brevity:

"Here are the two best prayers I know: 'Help me, help me, help me,' and 'Thank you, thank you, thank you.'"

You are saying those prayers over and over again as you listen to the whistle of the train pulling away, bound for the land of hope and dreams

TONY NATELLI

ABOUT THE AUTHOR

Kraig Scattarella

STEVE DUIN, 50, is the Metro columnist at *The Oregonian*, where he has worked since 1980. He has three children, two relatively worthless English degrees from Wake Forest University and one dauntless wife, Nancy, of 23 years. He is the co-author of three books: *Comics: Between the Panels,* a history of comic books; *Blast Off,* a retrospective on vintage space toys; and *Indomitable Spirit: Life-changing Lessons in Leadership.*